BROODING

John Griswold, *series editor*

BROODING

Arias, Choruses, Lullabies, Follies, Dirges, and a Duet

MICHAEL MARTONE

The University of Georgia Press   *Athens*

© 2018 by The University of Georgia Press
Athens, Georgia 30602
www.ugapress.org
All rights reserved
Designed by Erin Kirk New
Set in Minion and Whitney
Printed and bound by Thomson-Shore
The paper in this book meets the guidelines for
permanence and durability of the Committee on
Production Guidelines for Book Longevity of the
Council on Library Resources.

Most University of Georgia Press titles are
available from popular e-book vendors.

Printed in the United States of America
22   21   20   19   18   P   5   4   3   2   1

Library of Congress Cataloging-in-Publication Data

Names: Martone, Michael, author.

Title: Brooding : Arias, choruses, lullabies, follies, dirges, and a
    duet / Michael Martone.

Description: Athens : The University of Georgia Press, [2018]
    | Series: Crux: The Georgia series in literary nonfiction |
    Includes bibliographical references.

Identifiers: LCCN 2017047722| ISBN 9780820353074 (pbk. : alk.
    paper) | ISBN 9780820353067 (ebook)

Classification: LCC PS3563.A7414 A6 2018 | DDC 814/.54—dc23
    LC record available at https://lccn.loc.gov/2017047722

These are for Mother and Dad, more or less.

Contents

BROODING

Keynotes

Single Ruby

I was and am a "Single Ruby." Not, alas, a "Double Ruby." I am referring to my status as a member of the National Forensic League, the NFL, now the National Speech and Debate Association, I suppose, because of the confusion with that other NFL. Yes, a speech and debate society that awarded various levels of achievement, the single ruby being the penultimate gem. It was the cross X debate category of competition that tripped me up from obtaining the double. I did not cotton to the questions debated, did not like the style of speech, the hyper litanies of evidence, and the tracking of argument on flowcharts. I preferred the individual categories—extemp, impromptu, dramatic and comedic interp, poetry, original oratory, after-dinner speaking, the last a kind of keynote address. So, full disclosure, I stand here before you a mere Single Ruby forensic expert, not the Double. Damn you, debate. Allow me then to present evidence of my credentials. Here on my lapel you will notice a slight device: a silver soft metal pin of the type that is often presented by organizations, fellowships, and associations, consisting of a vertical bar, a thin cylinder with a loop at the top, and there, slightly below, look, the octagonal logo of the NFL with the single ruby winking in the sinister NFL stamped on the bend. These are strange little trinkets, aren't they? These honorary badges to indicate initiation into clubs, leagues, fraternities. On my campus, the engineering, business, and chemistry honorary societies have taken these little devices and enlarged them to gargantuan size and set them in stone like Arthurian swords, monuments of these strange, twisted bits of metal.

Those lapel pins—perhaps you all have one or two—evolved from a type of key. If you were a member of Key Club you were presented with a Key Club pin that was a stylized and streamlined key.

Once these keys were functional, the loop on top attaching it to a pocket watch chain. Phi Beta Kappa there displayed on your vest. The key's proximity to the pocket watch, a clue even as it evolved into a boastful fob. These abstract devices, once actual keys to wind that pocket watch, now vestigial appendages.

So this, then, is the first key of this stem-winding keynote speech about keys.

The Treasure House

It was called the Treasure House, the house Captain Kangaroo inhabited. *Captain Kangaroo*, a television show for children begun in the year of my birth. Running in the mornings, it broadcast on CBS in various forms until 1984. It opened with keys, I remember, keys that as they danced in the Captain's hands did not make music but cued music, a bouncy jingle that jingled as long as the Captain agitated the keys. They were big old keys on a big metal ring. The music skipped along. The sound of the keys underneath the jaunty theme lisped and stuttered until the Captain hooked the ring on a nail in the side of a big cabinet where later the puppets Bunny Rabbit and Mr. Moose would gyre and gimbal. The key ring placed on the nail. Silence. The Captain would lift the ring off the nail. The music would take up where it left off. On the hook. Silence. Off. The bouncy theme bounced around the Treasure House. This was thrilling. This narrowly defined tolerance between noise and nothing. I held my breath. The lesson of suspense. It was as if the ring and not the keys were the key to this, the switch that switched. I went back just now to watch this bit on old kinescopes only to discover something else. I had remembered incorrectly. I remembered the Captain opening the Treasure House with the musical keys from the outside but I was wrong. The door of the Treasure House was locked with a key on the inside, not the out.

A Hitch in Space and Time

From far above you see a vast foyer of a grand mansion. A party. People in formal evening dress being received. The camera, in a gliding descent, falls and falls, focusing on the hand in a fist held behind her back, now a close-up of her clenched fist, her hand that now opens. We see the key. The key in her palm now fills the screen. Years later. The conclusion of a television program has lodged in my mind. The program, first broadcast in 1979, was the American Film Institute's tribute to filmmaker Alfred Hitchcock. Ingrid Bergman, the evening's MC and the actor in *Notorious*, clutching the key, ends the night (is she wearing the same gown just pictured in the movie clip of that film?) with one final anecdote. She speaks to "Hitch," recounts the setup of the shot. Remember, she says, you built an elevator, a basket, you and the cameraman. The long shot, the close-up? And the cameras in the ballroom that night cut back and forth between Bergman and Hitchcock. She reveals now that the key captured there in her hand was, after the shot, stolen by Cary Grant, her costar, who kept it for ten years and who then, twenty years ago, gave it to me (Ingrid) to keep, saying it was a charm, had been good luck. She has kept it, this prop, not property so much as support, a spell, a spine, all these years. And now, another reveal. A close-up. She holds up that key, that key (like an exclamation mark), by its added string fob! The key! And she gives it back to Hitch saying, ironically (yes?), a joke, that it has brought me good luck, perhaps now it will open doors for you. She walks out into the sea of tables, to Hitch, holding up the key to give to him as if the key on its leash were leading her. Homing in on Hitch. The moment isn't about opening so much as it is about closure.

Arrowing

They are called, by the United States Postal Service, "arrow" keys. "Arrow" for the arrow that is conspicuously stamped on them. Their existence is a semisecret, perhaps just the stuff of legend now, but it makes sense. There should be just one key to all the locks that lock all the locked boxes overseen by the PO. The drop and relay boxes, the banks of apartment mailboxes, the safes and cabinets. Of course, there would be one key that opens and secures all of these portals. The letter carrier can't be carrying an individual key for each lock he or she interacts with each day. The arrow keys generate considerable anxiety. They are shrouded in mystery. A theft of one raises alarm. As it should, for the space it regulates, the border between the public space and the private, is fraught, though we forget. We forget that Hermes, the messenger, the godly postman, is also the patron of bankers and of thieves. He is found in the space between spaces, here in the neither here nor there. The arrow key fits the box that holds Schrodinger's cat. The arrow key "arrows," a key that opens that paradox of Zeno, the missile that can be proved never to hit its mark, moving by halves infinitely between the here and there, the now and then, the here and now, the there and then.

The Master Key

The master key was attached to a metal hoop that slipped over my head, worn like a noose or necktie, designed to keep my hands free to handle the luggage before roller bags. I was a night auditor at the Marriott, eleven to seven shift. I ran room and tax in the early early morning, balanced the house, working with only two other auditors, for the restaurant and bar, old-timers who had seen it all and made me, the kid, bellhop the bags of late check-ins. I wore the key ring around my neck all night as I keyed in numbers on the massive NCR 442, balancing out the folios for all 254 rooms whose spare keys needed to be found and fit back into the cubby slots behind the desk. The room keys still were tagged with plastic fobs that instructed the absent-minded customer to slip the key in any mailbox and it would be returned. Like a rosary, the master key had its loop I wore draped around my neck, a scapula, that bounced against my chest as I walked the fire walk through the halls, checked the water heaters for the blue pilot flame, with a little jingle, the belled cat as I prowled. The master key could even open the doors "pinned out," a method to force a guest to see the desk and settle accounts. In the morning, the big ring around my neck, I rang up rooms, made the wake-up calls at the PBX, fitting home the cord into its socket, toggling the ring. We had a crazy alarm clock that could be set every fifteen minutes. This was all analog, of course. And back then Marriott had a policy that if the call wasn't answered someone had to go and use the master key, make sure the business trader would not miss that meeting. Most times the guest was already gone, or in the shower, the television too loud. Due diligence done. The old-timers always made me go, reminding me that suicides always left wake-up calls. They didn't want to be saved, just found. The key thumping on my blazer. My heart thumping there. I'd find the room and knock and when there was no answer remove the ring from around my neck, seize the key, fit it in the lock, open the door (and it would always open) and look inside.

Walking Deadman

You will find them still in old office buildings, industrial lofts, warehouses. You will mistake them for antique bottle cap openers. They've been painted over, the stamped legend DETEX WATCHCLOCK STATION on the lid, melting into the paint on top. That enameled lid covers a little cast metal cup. An ashtray? An outlet cover? A fount for holy water? If you are luckier still, you can hinge that lid open and, with still more luck, find inside some type of key, a key attached to a heavy-duty chain riveted to the side of the receptacle. It is a jewel box with the key the jewel. They are near doors usually, the ends of hallways. You think the key has something to do with the nearby door but the chain does not reach. The strange key is leashed to an obsolete past. You have discovered a watch clock station, a part of an analog cybernetic system that married a man with a machine, a canteen-sized clock strapped over his shoulder. The watchman made his rounds, moved from station to station, lifting the lids and extracting the key found hidden there, keying each into the clock on his hip, the clock recording the time and his place in time. See, the readout would say, you were here, here, then here. The machine was a walking dead man. Proof that you moved and weren't asleep at your post, curled up like the key in some cubby. I look for them still these industrial cocoons and the keys that long ago wound up a watchman.

Gravity Works

It's so boring, watching a baby, a baby on the edge, just into the toddle, the toddler on the edge of everything, getting into everything. He must be watched constantly, and it is boring, this monitoring as the child tries, essays, everything over and over. We have developed a restraint. We call it a highchair and bundle the baby off to it. It looks downright medieval, this highchair with its belts and its sliding lipped tray table that pins him in to it. The baby, so encumbered, writhes and wriggles, all ampersands. We have learned to throw things onto the tray, distractions. Often it is cereal. It is almost always Cheerios. Why Cheerios, cheerless Cheerios? But it is, and the baby immediately responds, gasping and grasping, O-ing after the little o's. They are like little stemless keys, all thumbs, that he then inserts into any and all holes, tests the fit (nose, ears, eyes). Even as we begin to remember something about the hazard of choking, the kid has found where the Cheerios work. The mouth, yes, that's the ticket. And the child will commence to push all these buttons of oats down this open hatch. Then what do we do? We have played the Cheerio card. The baby looks up at us intently, a brown study of crumbs. And then we do it; we do it even when we know we shouldn't. We dig deep in our pockets and withdraw our key ring. Now here is an authentic choking hazard, but we are at our wit's end, too tired (and we can't leave him worming in that high chair) to go look for the oversized toothy teething keys (pastel-colored, soft-edged) designed and marketed for this very moment when we are about to serve up our real keys. The keys spread-eagle on the tray. Instantly, the child attempts to unlock this mystery (the empty vessel he is—ears, nose, mouth), scratching the tabula rasa of his still soft-spotted skull. Suddenly, he leans over, off to the side of the chair, and drops the keys. They fall, make a confused clatter on the kitchen floor. Then the baby does this: he looks at the keys on the floor. He looks at us. He looks at the keys. Us. We know what we are to do, what we will do. We pick up the keys and place them on the tray once more. And immediately they are once more on the floor. Again with the looking. Again with the picking up and the dropping. This can go on, it seems, for hours. "Gravity works," we cry out. But for the kid it doesn't. The next release the keys might drop up. The keys are key as they fall. As they fall they open for us, they open us (if we can just get past the tedium) to possibility. That space to wonder about wonder.

Hidden in Plain Sight

It seems I never carry cash anymore. Instead, money is the simple swipe transmission of the acrobatic magnetic zeros and ones from one virtual column to another. But now when I do carry a buck or two in my billfold for tips perhaps, or a vending machine, I still unfold the paper to look at the artwork and note all the changes in paper and printing to foil counterfeiting or to see if a message has been scribbled during the circulation but also I always look for the key. As a child you aren't entrusted with keys. The adults control the locks, the switches, the ignitions. I remember my father's key ring, pedestrian jewelry, in the bowl by the door with his change and wallet. And I remember the riddle as he removed the keys from the pile of his pocket detritus that remained: Find the key. There was a key in there someplace with the pocket knife (attractive and forbidden), the broken roll of Lifesavers, the scraps of paper and receipts, the pencil nub, the crumbled bills. He twirled the keys on his finger. It's in there he said. I looked and looked for this key, the treasure now and not the key to the treasure. I turned the wallet inside out—the photos and the mass cards, the phone numbers and the business cards, everything became then a thing itself, and I would look into the world of what was pictured, what was printed. And there, I found it on a dollar, one of many etched pictures and numbers—the sun-like seal of the Treasury and there almost an eyelash, the key not *a* key but *the* key. That key all these years later—my cookie, my madeleine—I scan for it in the rare dollar I dispense or receive. It opens me up as I unfold it. It reminds me. Turns something on in me. Now when I have change, I throw my it, *my change*, in the bowl by the door along with my keys, the poor contents of my pockets next to the depleted pile of my dead Dad's keys, keys that fit nothing any more but ignite, a persistent ring of objective correlatives, the little store of miniscule moments.

Key to Life

What did I know? I was just a kid really, twenty-three years old and living outside Indiana for the first time, a student for one year in Baltimore, in The Writing Seminars of Johns Hopkins. My mother, back home in Indiana, was happy to tell her friends she had a son at Hopkins, allowing those same friends to imagine that that son was on his way to being a doctor, not a writer. Writers were rare there, only two dozen in my class, but the Homewood campus was rife with doctors and those studying medicine, biology, science of all sorts, researchers mostly, the clinicians at the hospital on the other side of town. I fell in with one of them, Eric Nelson, who wrote poetry on the side. And who, when he learned I had never seen the Atlantic (or Pacific for that matter), insisted he show it to me, taking me "down the ocean," as they say, to camp on the beach at Chincoteague. We arrived at night and set up a tent in the dark, very near, I thought, a highway. The roar and whoosh of traffic over the dunes. I went to sleep clueless. In the morning, of course, that roar changed in the light, transformed into the busy Atlantic surf washing up on the beach. Eric let me hang out at his lab. This was only five years after the first recombinant DNA organism had been produced: an African clawed toad gene had been spliced into bacterial DNA. The place was giddy, the lab was learning how to unzip the helices of this or that gene, pick the locks of any molecule with the right enzymatic tool. I watched without seeing, really, as he shot a frog gene sequence into *E. coli*. And for a moment, he told me, there existed a new species, *E. coli nelsonenthis*. It didn't thrive. This was way before P3 labs or biohazard protective protocols. Who cared that we were gigging some gene in the guts of a bug that lives in every human gut? We were kids taking science out for a spin. Like that the world changed. Now you see it. Now you don't not.

Reliquary

I searched using the key words: relics, St. Nicholas, World Trade Center, nine eleven. To no avail. I must have dreamed this: the priest on the mound of rubble of the South Tower piled on the ruin of what had been the Greek Orthodox Church of Saint Nicholas, looking for the church's altar reliquary and the relics kept inside. A church's relics, the enduring bits of bone, the stains of blood, the splinter of the True Cross, are the key to the church's ignition switch. Its consecration on the dashboard altar charges the church, changes it from a secular space to a sacred one, a key fit into its casket snug in its stone. And it was this image of a priest scrambling over the wreckage of that day that lodged in my mind along with all the other images indelibly inscribed in bits and bytes. While scores of others searched through the ground-down ground of Ground Zero, recovering the remains, the remains of the newly martyred, the horrific forensic evidence, and, yes, the new relics of the dead, this priest was looking for old bones, evidence of the persistence of catastrophe and hope with all its benign evil. He needs to find the right relics in this vast landscape of relics. I think of this now every time I misplace my keys in the clutter and neglect of the things I have accumulated. The frustration of not being able to proceed, go forward, do anything until this sliver of cheap metal is back in my hands. As I search I think of that search and the way tiny keys turn everything—time and space—inside out as they turn in the lock. And I think of Elizabeth Bishop's line about how losing isn't hard to master and how she rhymes that word, with sorrowful irony and paradox, with disaster.

Transition Object

Hands behind the back. Men, mainly, as they stroll on the *volta*. They are working something in their hands. You can hear the chatter and click too if you are close enough. That tapping tsk. Worry beads being worried. *Komboloi*, the string trinket, can be found everywhere in the street markets and souvenir shops of Greece, as Greek, maybe, as souvlaki, ubiquitous as *matia*, the sea-blue evil eye, as iconic as amputated marble, beady-eyed icons. Not religious these beads. Usually sliding freely on a looped string the width of two palms, organic materials—coral, shell, amber—thought to be more handy to handle, though I have a stainless steel set in my pocket. Odd number of beads, usually one more than a multiple of 4, say 4 times 4, say. You worry the worry beads, thread them through the fingers, pinch and count them, toss them tethered (a little flip) and feel them spill back into your palm. While you talk, while you stroll, while you lean, while you think, while you figure, while you try to forget, try to remember. Remember. You let your fingers do the walking while you walk. You are working a combination, attempting to find the correct manipulation not to open something up so much as to unlock calm, to quiet. No playground of the devil these busy hands. In a pinch, a set of keys will do, a poor substitute, you know. Something to fiddle with. Fidget through. Metal conductors of that nervous energy. The hands that hold the keys, manipulate them, finger exercises, the hands, little complex engines complexly purring, idling with intent or indifference. Worrying worry. Worry worrying. This transition object like that lock of hair you twirl, thread through your fingers, the cheek you scratch, the ear you pull. You are here and you are elsewhere. Your fingers, your hands are negotiating the transition between, easing the separation from, unlocking the geared and flanged repetitive mechanism of fret, faint, feint, fright. The tumbling tumblers of worry.

G♯-Minor Seventh in the Second Inversion

Word has just reached us here in Tuscaloosa that in Halberstadt, Germany, two pipes have been removed from the Blokwerk organ in St. Burchardi Church, silencing a pair of E's that had been contributing to a chord playing continuously for the last year and a half. The keys are struck and stuck in that position by lead weights. The newly created chord will play until sometime in the year 2008. This is but a fragment of the 639-year concert of John Cage's opus called *As Slow as Possible*. Now the new note will sound for eighteen more months, I hear. Cage is most famous for the way he orchestrates the extremes of music. His chamber work *4'33"* consists, of course, of a performer or performers sitting in silence for four minutes and thirty-three seconds. *As Slow as Possible* began with twenty months of silence, or, more exactly, a rest where the only sound was the panting of the organ's electric bellows. I am fond of this admittedly highly conceptual piece. I admire its hopeful nature, its assumption that someone not only will be around to play the final notes of the coda but also that someone will be around to hear the silence that follows. The movements last seventy-one years each, lifetimes. There will be others present, as time goes on, to sound and sustain the decades-long chords, to harmonize with the apparently endless tonic, to engage the score for scores and scores of years.

I think about that newly constructed chord (sounding, still sounding) often. Listen, I live near trains. And their timely and timeless concerts seem to be a kind of folk version, an unselfconscious rendition of the avant-garde tooting going on in Germany.

I live near the old Southern mainline, the fertile crescent that connects New York to New Orleans and near what once was the marshaling yard of the L&N, where long drags—that's what they are called—of freight cars arrive, are broken apart, reassembled, and depart for Mobile or the Midwest.

I said I live near trains but the truth is we all live near trains. We've learned to ignore them, don't really take notice of them as they shuffle along their corridors of ruins, not until we are inconvenienced at a crossing where they emerge out of some back lot of history and obsolescence. Or maybe you still notice the sound trains make. More likely, their ambient industrial music, too, has been naturalized, filtered efficiently by your attentions, the sound suppressed, sidetracked.

Anytime a train moves or stops moving, it sounds its horn, little coded melodies that can be read, deciphered, stitched into a fragment of a phrase. A shave and a haircut. Two bits. Another visitation from some long-gone cultural past. Down in the yard right now there is a duet going on, a kind of melancholy argument probably between the local switch engine and the road engine just arriving from Vicksburg. Muted schwas wah-wahing and wailing, each trying to find a kind of final punctuation.

The contemporary compressed air horns, still pitched in the low minor key of the earlier steam whistle, are less expressive. In steam, the engineer could show his hand, slow his hand, manipulate the duration and dynamic, the warble and waver with a tug of a cord. The modern horn has less play, hobbled by its binary toggle switch, slightly less soulful. But still. The notes reaching me now from the main line are still that ancient concocted cocktail bawling. In fact, that long throat-clearing burst, clearing the tracks, is the first note of a highballing varnish expediting southward, just entering the urban pas de deux. And even in the joy of going, the note lingers endlessly, depressed and amped up, all the way through town, warning, crossing after crossing, of its crossing, pushing the sound ahead of it, a gulp and another blast, hiccupping as it glides into the station on Greensboro Avenue.

How strange to have this music always there. Background. Foiled and foiling. It saturates the air everywhere. Disembodied and massive, a moving wall, a kind of static, yet with distant distinct eruptions of a phrase, a fragment that first asserts then loses its train of thought. Transmitted through invisible air, the hidden source is most often on the move, restless, remote, receding, leaving this polyphonic note floating in a wake. The sound has no origin. It just seems to spring. Silence warped to sound. A steaming streaming auditory geyser.

For a long time in its schedules Amtrak printed a little footnote about the procedures for transporting human remains on their trains. The sounds trains make were meant to warn or communicate mundane information, signals before the wireless, but those practical sounds morphed even then into our constant ululation, our wallpaper keening, our diesel funeral dirge, our mechanical Muzak of mourning. It is the perfect accompaniment, hard now to distinguish that sound from our general, sustained, steeped sadnesses. It is seamlessly incorporated into our emotional wiring, our ambient ache. The sound from the tracks our bereft looping soundtrack.

Time coming at you. Time leaving you behind. The Doppler yodel emanates from the hulking shadow racing with it, hard on its heels there where the Southern cross the Dog. It is a warning that gets swallowed up by a sigh, a sob, and somewhere out there, forever after, the silence.

Titled: The Title

A Short Short Story's Own Short Short Story

I write long, long titles for my short short stories. I suppose this is, for me, existential, a function of the genre, a genre that defines itself, first, with this intensified brevity—the *short* short. But what kind of brevity? What is the quality of briefness? The shortness of the short, the short shortness has, most often, to do with word count, and also (though less often) with the word count's relationship with page length, and, by extension, the number of pages. I have noticed that the genre's most definite defining instruction found in the guidelines for contest and anthology solicitations spell out the length of "short." It seems length is perhaps our only agreed-upon convention. Adrift in the miasmic nebulousness of this form it is comforting to count beans, to have beans to count on. The prompt to write this something we call the short short story is addressed in terms of numbers of words—250, 500, 1,000—or numbers of pages—one page or complete on these two facing pages: often the only defining characteristic of the short short story is this kind of length, or lack thereof, and at the very least length as a defining characteristic goes a long way, a kind of essential DNA, as close as we get to formula, or rules.

I believe this piece here was to measure out at 2,000 words (or so I remember). Yes, 2,000 words. But let me burn some of those words on this aside. Just how quaint, how antique to use that particular scale of numbers—250, 500, 1,000—numbered for such metrics for this genre of short fiction, already strange because the genre is already mostly characterized by word count, page count, but so curious also that the word count, page count, is still based on the ancient typewritten page of 250 words. This makes me think that the form, perhaps, is a creature, most of all, not of the handwritten page but the typewritten page or of the computer-written page—the computer hobbled to act like the antiquated nineteenth-century machine. I am at this moment using double-spaced Courier on my iMac to mimic the typewriter and the 250-word page. All of this to say that this is a lot of words to say this: if an essential part of the form is the formal limitations of words, and every word counts in the form, then do the number of words in the title count in the count?

I like to think when I think about word count that the words floating at the top of this column don't count. That the words in the title inhabit a kind of duty-free zone of existence, the realm of untaxed perfume and spirits, a transient space unencumbered where one passes through, where one is nowhere and everywhere. The title is like the hidden text of the computer page, that 50% gray ghost print. The title, like the headers and footers, is para-text, graying in the gray area, so when whatever editorial assistant sits down to count the words to see if this or that piece is the right kind of short to be a short short story, he or she will start with the "I" with which this essay started and regard the title starting with "Titled" as a kind of gimme, a practice swing, a tune-up, a fumbling focus, throat clearing, tuning fork tabulation it is and it isn't. Now, the computer is not so forgiving. This word here, this "here" is word 600 according to the meter running at the bottom of the frame of this open window, and embedded in that number 600 are the 11 words of the title. I have used over 600 words, one way or another, to get to this point, right here, all to say only that titles, whether they count or not in the accountancy of word count rules, count. And because we most often take titles for granted, they're granted to us. We don't grant to them much of the much more they could be.

Where is it written that we as writers need to title what we write? It is a convention so deeply ingrained as to be invisible to us. The practice, no doubt, reaches back to some primordial primary grade school lesson of composition writing by rote. "Now class begin your paper with a 'title' and remember to center your title on the first line . . ." Yes, there are the experiments of avoiding the imperative of the title, titling the title "Untitled" or titling with cardinal or ordinal numbers that now can incorporate the digital dot to the various versions—Title 2.0—to the numeric sequence. Yes, the generic "Poem" and the more rare "Story" or "A Story" have been used, but they are still titles even as they resist title-ness, and yes, even the Dickensonian blankness that is left blank gets filled by the default of the first line that follows the purposeful nothingness. The text abhors this vacuum. Tide and title rushes in.

For the prose writer, the title is as close as he or she will get to writing a poem. The poem loves to play close in the valence of individual words and

the multiple meanings, sometime contradictory, meanings the word embodies as well as the lubricated surfaces of the several such words rubbing up
against one another. The example I love is from Auden and his partial line:

Poetry makes nothing happen

in which the pressure is all over the word "nothing" and the simultaneity of
its making "makes nothing happen" and "nothing happen" a force forcing
the reader to inflect with personal emphasis the English spin on this particular cue. The poem can have us, has had us, read (at least) both ways of
reading, reading at the same time and as well as sequentially backward and
forward, the exact inexactness of the sense. A poem and a title, I am arguing
here, fights against the existential nature of the medium of prose that insists
the words line up, be read in order and with a syntax that yanks the kinks
out of convolution. A poem and here a title are ones to be inhaled all at
once, a fast-acting pill dissolving. Like a painting, poetry is a wall of sense
and sense and senselessness that is at once centered and in the periphery.
The title, this kind of poem, does not so much participate in the stylistic
ideal of the prose it precedes. It is not interested in transparency, a clear
window transmission of the content. Instead the title hedges. It is a thicket,
a bramble, a roll of concertina wire. It contains one thing and at least one
thing more, and it contains the one thing and all of the everythings the
piece title titles is not. If the story is a maze one works one's way through on
the path of pea gravel, the title is the maze's maze, all topiary all the time.

The picture postcard's stamp is the picture postcard's picture postcard.
Stamps are highly elaborated works of art we routinely carry around, often
overlooked as our attention is focused upon the thing "underneath" the
scribbled greeting or the view out the vacation window. The title too is frank
franking, a stamp to validate and is cancelled. It shares with the card, its
affixing in fact animates the card, the last piece, a kind of key that propels it
through the world. But at the same time the stamp and the title remain aloof
separate from the thing it's attached to. It has its own aesthetic. The title is
both symbiotic and autonomic, its vision is both binocular and depthless, a
gem seen through a jeweler's loop.

A long title at the beginning of a very short story alerts in a reader's mind
not so much the meaning, theme, or content of the prose but the slant notion
of scale itself. A short short story may be about a lot of things but one thing

it is always about is scale. It is about the strategy of concentration, compaction, compression, as if the prose were being squeezed by some piston to the point of spontaneous combustion. The title then works to machine this shrinkage. You work through the title like a sieve, a filter. Negotiating a title recalibrates you to this new world you are about to end no longer metered in meters but now in microns or angstroms. The title acclimates you through its distortions to the distortions to come, a zoom lens attached to the microscope.

How small is small finally? An element, say, or the atoms inside the elements or the nucleus and electron shells inside the atom, the particles inside the protons and electrons, the particles of particles, the small that is finally undetectable. How long is a short story? How short is it to be? How long is the title, this other entity that orbits the thing it titles. Is it a satellite, a moon, a belt of dust? Or can the story be a collapsed star, dense and deep, that the story in its flight is hinged upon? The title perhaps is the still center that snaps the story around, indeed, the story must be read in full to finally unlock the meaning of the title. The title not a simple introduction at all but the question posed for the story to answer. Perhaps the short short story we always write is the title. And the fall of letters from the title down the page like a curtain of matrix of stars is nothing more than an over-large enabling apparatus for the few words of the title? As a writer of the short short story my desire is by definition to be short as possible, short squared. So what can be shorter than a title? The short short story's short short story. That next step toward the shortness that in its even less-ness is next to godliness.

Brooding

Seventeen years ago. The house in Syracuse, on Fellows Avenue. A sun porch on the second floor, windows all around, she had painted a pencil yellow, a school bus yellow. The squat computer, a putty color, sat on the sterilizer table, dialed up, squawked for the first time. Tone and twinkle, hiss and static sigh, ripping zip, twist and ratchet. O. O. O. "Hello."

@

In the cloud of trees, canticles of cicada barked, waxed, and waned, tinkered with their tuning.

@

stillness
penetrating the rock
sound of cicada
                    —Basho

@

Lycos . . .
Magellan . . .
Excite . . .
Northern Light . . .
Alta Vista . . .
Yahoo!!!
Netscape . . .

@

May. Now. Seventeen years later, Brood II emerges in the east.

@

Magicicada Septendcim
Magicicada Septendecula
Magicicada Cassini.

@

Cicada, cicada, cicada. The name (though it is not onomatopoeic but Latin for "tree cricket") mimics the song. The long sibilant. The cawing caw. The dada da of the of the of the denouement, a trill falling off, entropic, unable to escape the gravity of, of, of a marble, dribbling on, each rebound lessening, dribbling on a concrete floor.

@

Just now, just now (another window is open on this machine, a program running) the chirrup of an alert. As I type this "this," a comment has emerged in my timeline. The comment palimpsesting into place on the Facebook. Two tones, two tones like like the clicking cricket the nuns (I remember) used to use to time our genuflections.

@

a cicada chirrs—
there! and there!
stars appear
          —Issa

@

One billion buried grubs per square mile. Buried for seventeen years but not asleep, no, no suspended animation, no dreaming dreams of waking, of falling upward. A lot of rooting around down there. Rooting for roots. The earth crawling with them, coiled like the watch springs they are.

@

All one needs to do is type into a field and enter. In seconds, millions of returns return in seconds, scores and scores of hits, hints from hither and yon, hinterlands come out of hiding. The lists and lists come back in instants and after years one wonders no longer about an other, another one. Another other emerges. Emerges.

@

Now that I think about it, the @, the "at" symbol, the ampersat, that balled-up bug, has the look of a burrowing, bulging-eyed nymph. Or the @ is a map of absence. A sink of seeking. A sink of sought. All that time circling down the drain. Screwed. Worm-holed. Bored and bored.

@

Then, the elm trees were still living, and they were scaled with the spent shells, the papered and papery leavings the bugs bugged out of. I had to pry them from the trunks they were stuck to. Pointing up the brick siding of my grandparents' red brick house as well, grappled in the grout, a kind of fossil ivy. I kept them in a glass jar, a mess of little brittle blisters, those bugged-out eyeless eyes, blown glass, goo goo googly, bulging orbits. Shifting shifts. Slit-open sleeves. A thousand thousand-yard stares. What were they thinking? Thought balloons configuring their own empty empty-headedness. And all around me, invisible, was the busy full-bodied buzz buzz babbling of the brooding.

@

"Do you know the legend about cicadas? They say they are the souls of poets who cannot keep quiet because when they were alive, they never wrote the poems they wanted to."

—John Berger

@

a cicada shell
it sang itself
utterly away
—Basho

@

I wonder what happened to her or her or her. Carol Clay Clay Clay. The scuffed anthills on the walks home from school. Nancy Carrollllllll. The lightning bugs made into ashy jewelry. Maripat Golf, an estuary of silence after that graduation party in somebody's backyard, where after seeing her through the screen of the lilac bush, obscenely in bloom, touch David Ecenbarger's hand (I've looked him up—he's dead, he died after that but before this writing now) I ran back home through the alleyways of North Highlands and the tunnels of screaming sirens, cicadas sawing, seeing what

I saw again and again. Where are you now? You and you and you. Why after all these years can this song or that one or this one here not be unsung?

@

"Over the course of an emergence, male periodical cicadas congregate in huge choruses or singing aggregations, usually located high in trees. Females visit these aggregations and mate there. Males of all species have typical calling songs as well as special courtship songs, the latter being given only in the presence of females. In *Magicicada septendecim*, the calling song is a prolonged buzz that drops in pitch at the end: *weeeeeee-ah*. This song is very low pitched around 1.3 kHz . . . When a male approaches a female, she responds by clicking her wings after each song, and he slurs his songs together."
          —*The Songs of Insects* by Lang Elliott and Wil Hershberger

@

I stare at my screens. Images of zombies back from the dead staring back at me. I believe I am to identify with the living in these dramas, but secretly I have much empathy for the reanimated dead. Their staring reminds me of my staring. Their predation of brains is done too literally, I think, for the sake of an audience's visceral response. I like to think of that hunger more metaphorically, a desire not for the biological nutrient but the virtual one. There is a mad curiosity I see. "What'd I miss?" Suspended underground, out of time, as you were, poor zombie. It is a hunger for the synaptic recording of time, the looping tapeworm of memory. The past needs to be tapped. Stare at me now, staring at this screen as I scroll through the searches, searching for what? What? What? My shuffling, stuttered scroll. My clicking. My stalling. My missing. My finding.

@

even with cicada—
some can sing
some can't
          —Issa

Hermes Goes to College

The First Thing

The very first thing the baby Hermes does is steal the cattle of Apollo, his brother. Apollo figures it out, confronts his baby brother, the little thief, in his crib. Hermes hasn't even learned to speak yet, to walk. The first thing he has to do is steal the sacred cattle of his brother Apollo, who figures it out and is about to extract terrible godly retribution for the transgression when Hermes offers up to his brother the second thing he does after he is born. He gives his older brother a little something he has been monkeying with while in the crib. He gives his brother the lyre—tortoise shell and horn and leather straps and string—so that all-seeing Apollo is charmed, calms down, can compose his great Apollonian art.

Confused on Purpose

Robert Scholes, in his little book *Elements of Fiction*, roots out that both fact and fiction derive from the Latin "to do" or "to make." A fact—the real thing—is a thing done. In fact, fact has no reality once it is done. It has no existence, is unreal. It leaves instead an abundance of residue, evidence, traces, the fact of its once having been done. A fiction, on the other hand, is a thing made, and once it is made it comes into existence. It has a reality. It can be sensed, stored, savored even. Fictions in this way are realer than facts whose evidence of the facts' doneness—letters, say, or reports, newspaper dispatches, diaries, etc.—can all be faked. The truth is for a very long time we have been operating as if fact and fiction were steady and distinct categories when in fact . . . And all that evidence of fact—the material of the real—can be faked, of course. We are really always already quite confused anyway.

The Genre of Genre

I am worried that we don't worry enough about the subliminal influences of the institutions in which we find ourselves housed, colleges and universities, which for me seem to be diabolical engines for sorting, categorizing, defining. If you think about it, the kind of writing my writing students are most engaged in is criticism, specifically the critique of fellow students' creative writing. The institution is a critical institution and insists we act critically. We want to think of such influence as benign, but it is not. We have adapted our writing, this writing, to the academic model, to the critical turn of mind. It must be seen as serious, empirical, enlightened. Even now in this essay, in this collection of essays that is interested in blurring the lines of genre, we still must use words like "genre." We are interested in the confusion of genre, the borrowing of technique between the genres, the tension that exists as one genre rubs up against the other. But still we are quite conscious and quite ready to admit to the easy use of "genre" altogether. We worry the categories of fact and fiction. Nonfiction and fiction. Prose and poetry. What we don't worry well enough is the category of category, the genre of *genre*.

The Art of Inconvenience

To invoke "literary" or "genre" is to create a frame where something can be made safe. It is a kind of precinct, a ghetto, even. Writers in America seem to have voluntarily committed themselves to some kind of reservation—the university—and assigned their work to very controlled publishing venues— the literary journal, the little mag, the peer-reviewed periodical. Now, there are many very nice, tasteful, serious literary journals, etc., but I can't help thinking that one thing these publishing venues are signaling the world is this: this this, this published this, is harmless, tamed, framed, controlled. And that this fiction, this nonfiction, this art, is not really a part of your life, dear reader. This is a zoo you can visit. I like art in its natural habitat, in the wild. Or if it is in the journals, it is acting like a bug, a germ, resistant to the antibiotic. Art that doesn't know its place. Art out of place. Art that disrupts convention, corrupts expectations. I like the notion of defamiliarization, of attempting to open up received notions and categories to wonder or to, at least, satire. I like art that appears in settings not thought to be artistic, not sanctioned precincts of appreciation. At the crosswalks and the crossroads. Contested spaces.

Outside the warehouses of the galleries and the tasteful storage sheds of the literary journal. The prank and the stunt. Art that is inconvenient, that disrupts, that by its nature corrupts, degrades, disturbs boundaries instead of politely sharing, tweaking, or bending them. Art not generically generic genre.

Meet John Smith

I attended a massive state university where it was a widely held belief that each student there was no more than a number. So, with only a made-up social security number we created a student, John Smith, and registered him by means of then-current IBM punch cards acquired at the field house registration. Tuition was cheap then, and everyone in my dorm, whose population was larger than most towns of the state, chipped in a buck or two. We enrolled him in large lecture classes—someone from the dorm was taking the class and shared the notes with the one who took the exam as John Smith. He was a C student. He did not attend the commencement held at the huge stadium and is now on the rolls of the alumni association, where he still receives the magazine at the P. O. Box we opened for him and maintain in Oolitic, Indiana. Sure, I realize with advanced software, heightened anxiety of identity theft, and terrorist breeches of security, and the cost of college now actually an arm and a leg instead of twenty bucks a semester hour, such a stunt would be impossible today. Or maybe not—one could hack the system virtually now and not have to worry about anything physical at all, but that is a thought for another day.

A Warning Warning

Today I teach at a massive state university where the regulation of vehicular and pedestrian traffic captures our attention. There is a sign, a giant yellow diamond warning, that pictures the international symbol of a human walking. You know these signs alerting you to a crosswalk, and you probably know the ongoing editing of the sign, its evolving story. One day you discover a sketched-on undulating hula-hoop ovaling the waist of the stick figure. That then is erased by the DOT. Then circles are stenciled to the feet, roller skates, that are, in a day or two, painted back over. A halo or horns added to the head. Or trailing lines indicating speed or sweat or blood or comic nerves, the shakes. A cast and a sling appear and are expunged. A red reflective button nose. Wings and goggles. And all the time the maintenance crews come back to set it all back in order. The warning warning sign must merely warn, while art, on the other hand, warns against such maintenance.

Reader's World

All through college I worked for a bookstore called, really, Reader's World, and Reader's World, like most bookstores divided its floor of product into categories of genre—the wall of fiction with its subdivisions of western, sci-fi, lit, and romance, and the expanse of nonfiction breaking into such groups as gardening and home repair, biography, war, psychology and therapy, self-help and how-tos, true crime and nature, travel and religion. Here is a secret of what I learned in Reader's World. Readers are not generic in the usual sense. That is to say their cognitive maps organizing information do not correspond with the one in the store or the one in the university for that matter. The primal division for my customers was not fiction and nonfiction but story and not story. Real or not, factual or not. These were questions, certainly, but not of primary importance. Consider that the Reader's World I worked in was located in a shopping center called Canterbury Green, the boxes of the various stores gussied up in fake timber and wattle and asbestos tile that was meant to look like thatch. Consider too that while I worked at Reader's World I shelved a brand new magazine called *People*, and I remember trying to figure out where to place it on the rack on the spectrum from the tabloids, enjoying their first flush of upwardly mobile success, to *Time* and *Newsweek*. The customers seemed to live comfortably in this in-between state. And the conflation of fact and fiction—one I think today is even more pronounced—was collapsing from both ends of the range. Books popular while I worked at Reader's World included *Ragtime* by Doctorow, a fictional animation of history, Mailer's *The Executioner's Song*, reportage expanded by fictional devices, Toomer's *Cane*, and Hong Kingston's *Woman Warrior*, a book so blatantly both fiction and non and about the very subject of genre as to make it unclassifiable. And, in fact, we spent the summer moving our copies of *Woman Warrior* from one area of the store to another and then leaving copies, a few copies of the title, in each of several sections, salting the whole store.

Stealing Things In

I have my students in both my fiction and nonfiction classes make books and distribute them as part of the semester's project. Book is a category that is in decay here. I have had a student write a story in the form of a police report, and he filed it as a police report at the police headquarters. Another student wrote a sequence of prose poems on the subject of meat. Her book, bound in blood red wrappers with a bone white spiral spine, she then took to the Winn Dixie to have shrink-wrapped on a Styrofoam tray by the butcher there. And still another hand-printed his story, about a character who uses a thirty-foot strip of sized cloth to floss his GI track, on a thirty-foot strip of sized cloth. But most do books that look like books, keeping Kinko's busy with standard staple folds and cardstock covers. I point out to them, as they have to distribute their books as well, that libraries and bookstores have elaborate apparati to prevent you from stealing a book out of their stacks but they have nothing to guard against you stealing your work into the bookstore or the library. And that's what they do, shelving their own work or leaving it to be shelved, allowing the librarian to affix the catalog number, enter it into inventory.

Hermes Clueless

So after reading this essay, we go back to our cribs. Do we go back there knowing more? Do we return having learned something or other? I'd like to think we have come here to unlearn. That's not to say "forget," but to return in a state of not-knowing. Once the contraption of tortoise shell and horn and leather strings fell into the hands of Apollo he knew what to do with the lyre. Open up a music department and study the heck out of the thing till it reveals its secrets—its bone, its horn, its leather. Hermes had no idea what his hands created save maybe an improvised distraction, the sleight of hand, of a thief. He's the artist, clueless, making something new out of those old received categories of bone and horn and skin, out of those old scraps and odds and ends, something new in the world. Make things. Steal them into the world.

Hat Trick

Hatless President

It is widely believed that American men stopped wearing formal hats—fedoras and bowlers, homburgs and boaters—when President Kennedy showed up at his inauguration without a top hat. That is not wholly accurate. Hat sales to men did collapse during Kennedy's administration, and Kennedy did not like wearing hats. But there are photographs of Kennedy in a top hat on his way to the Capitol. Lyndon Johnson, Kennedy's successor, was the first hatless president, though being a Texan he did wear Stetsons but not at his inauguration. All of this might be a kind of historic echo—a president's fashion dictates the dress of the nation. The rise of the Panama hat (a soft straw fedora made in Ecuador, where in 1944 the hats were that nation's primary export) was attributed to another president, Theodore Roosevelt, when he sported one while operating the controls of a steam shovel at the eponymous canal.

The Straw Hat Riot

The Straw Hat Riot took place in New York City, beginning on September 13, 1922, two days before the unofficial date when men were to switch from their summer straw hats to their winter felts and silks. The riot lasted a week. It involved thousands. There were many injuries and arrests. Countless crushed straw hats. It had been brewing for years. The city's haberdashers hired boys to knock the straw hats off any delinquent wearer of the same after the fifteenth, the conventional, silently agreed-upon day of conversion, in order to assure new purchases, spur the economy. There is a straw-hat day in the spring as well, though no one now remembers it. These public anniversaries are fading in the collective memory—the "no white after Labor Day" kind of rule—as are all the occasions of occasional "dress." Uniforms. Work, school, church clothes. Formal, casual, sport attire. Even the keeping of a complete wardrobe seems beside the point. We now have nice clothes, clothes always being described as "comfortable." It is hard to imagine riots over a hat, that hats would be, well, political, but in 1920s mobs were snatching and smashing straw hats all over Manhattan.

How You Gonna Keep Them down on the Farm

This semester I taught once more a class called Contemporary Rural and Agricultural Literature. I started teaching the course in the 1980s when I worked in Iowa and the farming debt crisis was in full swing. I grew up in a city, Fort Wayne, and knew little about the farms that were all around me. I knew even less about the conditions of the crisis in which farms now seemed to be entering. When I taught the class in Iowa, my students were from farms and rural towns. Later when I held classes on the same subject at Harvard, Syracuse, and Alabama, outside of Iowa, nearly everyone was two or three or more generations from a farm. I ask these students to draw a picture of a farm and a farmer the first day. The results are pretty uniform. The farm consists of a big haymow barn with silo, lots of animals, a windmill, a two-story house with a porch (gothic windows!) and picket fence to keep the chickens scratching in the yard penned up. The farmer is always the same—a man in denim bib overalls, a hayfork or hoe in hand, a full frayed brim straw hat, and, always, something, a straw of some kind, in his mouth. Over the term the class addresses two matters. First, that farms and farmers don't look this way anymore and second, why is it that we think they do or, more precisely, why is it we want them to look like those depicted in the drawings? Right now, I just want to think about that hat, that wide-brimmed worn-out straw sun hat. It is true that if you look at pictures from the Great Depression praising famous men, Farm Security Administration documentary photos, you'll see that hat and all kinds of full-brimmed fedoras as standard head gear of field work. But when I started teaching the class in the eighties, that hat had been replaced by the polyester-fabric-plastic-mesh-and-solid-six-paneled-one-size-fits-all-foam-billed-plastic-adjustable-back-tabbed baseball cap. It was known as a "gimme." I tried, back then, to track down its origin. Most Iowans I talked to believed it was created first by Pioneer Hi-Bred, a seed company founded in 1926 in Des Moines by FDR's vice president Henry Wallace. It came in the company's trademarked green color, sporting an embroidered patch of the company's logo a lazy infinity symbol, sprouting a corn sprout at its pinched waist. The hat was cheap to make and indestructible and, back then, retained a sense of the modern, optimistic future as agri*culture* began to think of itself as agri*business*. The hat was a kind of early bling as well. You got to sport the colors of a first-class scientific, international operation, a professional kind of uniform to replace the raggedy dungarees. There were other branded freebies—coats and gloves. It was the marriage of social realist workers' propaganda to capitalist irreal advertising. That marriage set up a contest between the two teams, competing lifestyle lives. It had only been twenty years before the donning of the seed cap that Soviet Premier Nikita Khrushchev had famously visited the Garst farm. That seed cap seeded the whole—the co-op cap, the implement cap, stockyard, dairy, fertilizer cap followed. This representing represented a profound shift. The clothes that clothed the new complex relationship between the free-holding landholders and their ever-expanding corporate and capital-concentrating "partners" as being on one big team. But it was also a disguise. That blingy brands wearing quickly transformed its meaning, warping into another kind of "branding." The cap style, though, had legs and migrated via truckers into town, into the suburb and the city. The cap knocked off the campaign hats and peaked caps of cops, the barracks and garrison hats of soldiers and fry cooks, the pith helmet of postmen, the kepis of conductors, the tweedy soft caps of duffers, the sweat-stained trilbies of football coaches. All hats. This hat became *the* hat. It came to be seen as the great working-class chapeau. Men might not wear hats like they used to but they would wear, do wear, this hat. It was great for hiding baldness or a bad hair day. The rebel could wear its bill to the back or to the side. Soon it wore its brand but also the logo of its maker. The price tag left on as the "gimme" evolved to an expression of wished-for status, conspicuous consumption. It is so ubiquitous now as to be almost invisible. Or subliminal, as it always carries its billboard above its bill.

The Context of No Context

In his book *Within the Context of No Context*, George W. S. Trow wrote, in 1980, about his father's hat. His father wore a fedora without a second thought. Trow himself wore one trimmed with scare quotation marks, as it were. "Irony has seeped into the felt of any fedora hat I have ever owned—not out of any wish of mine," he writes, "but out of necessity. A fedora hat worn by me without the necessary protective irony would eat through my head and kill me." A hat is not only a hat. Its loss stood for the loss of the seriousness of purpose. The hat made sense in a context. Its loss is also a symbol of the demise of a controlling elite, a kind of fallen felt crown. The book is about more than hats. It is a lot about television, hatless television. Trow suggests that the world changed with the game show "Family Feud," the first game show where the right answer was not the right answer but the answer that most people (polled studio audience members) believed was the right answer. This shift he sees also in the contrast between the covers of the now-defunct *LIFE* magazine and its Time-Life spinoff, *People*. If you were on the cover of *LIFE*, Trow believed, it made you famous. If you were on *People*'s cover you were already famous. Mr. Trump, a creature of the frameless contexts of television and gossip, has brought back the hat. But not the felt fedora. He favors the branded baseball cap. That screen-printed "Make America Great Again," I see, now that he is elected, has given way to an embroidered U S A. I guess America is back now that it is on the front of the cap. Trow's fedora, Trow seems to have said, was a metaphor, an objective correlative. It stood for something. This new hat comes with its "meaning" printed on the escarpment of its crest, its own gloss. Its own Cliff's Notes.

Color Me Red

I was stymied in my attempt to find the official color of the "Make America Great Again" baseball cap. I think of it as red but what red? There must be an agreed-upon Pantone numbered color. I recently discovered that the official crimson for the University of Alabama and Indiana University is the same, Crimson PMS 201. As hard as I looked I could not find an exact numbered shade, though, on ordering forms for the hat. The customer was given a range of colors, a spectrum of Pantone hues to customize the hat. I think of the hat as red, but I also found an article speculating on the correlation between the mood of the candidate and the color of the hat he was wearing. White, the informant believes, indicates a buoyant mood, while red signals that we should take warning. I learned that the hat comes in black too. No speculation on what wearing that color would mean. You can order the cap with special embroidery—a general's golden scrambled egg garland on the bill. My search did discover that many sources attempted to assign a Pantone color to Mr. Trump's skin. The consensus seems to be a Pantone color called Gold Flame 16–1449 TPX. I guess "red" it is, the cap's color. I am colorblind so I don't really see it, the red of the red. I have to take Mr. Trump's word for it.

The Fit

I like hats. I wear hats. All kinds of hats. I noticed early on in the 2016 presidential election campaign that the candidates were, as usual, hatless, but in the absence of hats there is always hair, or the lack of it, to consider and comment upon. I remember reports of past political seasons posting pieces on haircuts and hair plugs, on the sides of severe parts and on liberal curls and conservative comb-overs, evil widow's peaks and Hollywood dye jobs. So it was curious when the one current candidate garnering the most commentary for his hair (his coiffure a concoction of Brutalist architecture and sketchy Escher-esque terracing) donned a hat. It made me think, that hat. The summer political conventions would soon be here, and I thought how those conventions, in my lifetime, had always featured a certain kind of hat, another kind of hat: the straw boater, not the baseball cap of the moment. True, as time went on, the boater's function as just a hat changed more into costume signifier, straw into pressed Styrofoam, of the ritualized political convention and ossified barbershop quartets. Still, the boater persisted as political attire. Its flat surfaces provide in the television age, I suppose, stages for decoration and display of stuffed donkeys and plush elephants and bands of buttons and a stand for flags. But through it all, the boater retains enough of a signature to read as a political hat, the hat that hosts political conventions. Strange. The boater was simply popular summer headgear from the late 1800s when conventions as we know them began, and they continued to be so until the Great Depression, when the boater was eclipsed by the soft straw Panamas. The boater would have been *de rigueur*, then, worn to those un-air-conditioned conventions held in field houses, stadiums, armories, amphitheaters, and "gardens." It is as close as we come to traditional costume, a civic uniform. I didn't have a boater. I do now. I ordered one online from the Gentleman's Emporium. I got the cheaper one, a softer Laichow straw, two-inch brim with a dandy grosgrain satin ribbon of navy and red folded into a bow. They also called it a skimmer, the boater, this kind of hat. As the presidential campaigns moved around the country, I followed the progress of my boater as it shipped, drifting from warehouse to distribution center, all the logistics. It arrived in a special box, the boater's crown nestled and suspended to prevent crushing in the transit. The lozenge cloth label sewn into the band reads "Authentic SCALA Classico" wreathed with "Dorfman Pacific Company" and "Handmade Since 1921." A less-elegant label is tacked behind it, digitally produced ideograms for "do not wash," "do not bleach," "do not dry," "do not iron." Do not iron? And "100% Laichow/Laichow, XLarge/X-Grande." The reverse has "Made in China/Hecho en China." I like it. It is like a fossil. A ruin. It is a historic artifact. It doesn't even seem to be a hat. It could be a planter, a wall decoration. It is out of time and space. And, indeed, its provider, Gentleman's Emporium, seems to do most of its business creating clothing and headgear for steampunk aficionados and anachronistic reenactors. Now I know how to see it, this hat. I see now that I possess the crucial piece of my postmodern attire, my posthistorical ensemble. The idea of progress is so last season. Going forward is not fashion forward after all. I always thought that a boater had transmuted into the sphere of costume—all tap dancey and vaudevillian. But if the suit fits, wear it, yes? All the world's a stage and all that. Costume consumes us. "History," said the boater-bedecked (or was it a bowler?) Henry Ford, "is all bunk." Or so we seem to remember. What he really said was "History is more or less bunk. It's tradition. We don't want tradition. We want to live in the present, and the only history that is worth a tinker's damn is the history that we make today." That sounds . . . familiar. Okay. Today, we have the detritus of costume and custom, scraps of quotations all scotch-taped together, straw men and paper dolls. Every day we put on some sort of suit, pieces pieced together. I lift the boater out of its box and flip it by the brim up over my head and lower it down on my crown. It fits. But what does that mean, it fits? And does it? And if the hat does fit how, how will I wear it?

Ostrakons at Amphipolis, Postcards from Chicago

Thucydides and the Invention and Deployment of Lyric History

K-4 Pacific vs. J-1 Hudson

Each night at Englewood Junction on Chicago's south side the Pennsylvania Railroad's Broadway Limited leaving from Union Station and the New York Central's 20th Century Limited leaving from LaSalle Street Station, both bound for New York City overnight, meet to race on their paralleling rights-of-way to the Indiana line.

He begins his History of the Peloponnesian War this way—"Thucydides, an Athenian wrote the history of the war . . ." but eases into the first person halfway through the paragraph. It is as if the tradition of invoking the muse has now transmuted to invoking the self. Is Thucydides the source or its receiver, the inspiration or the action, subject or object, the new or the news?

Time Begins in Chicago

Not far from here on the block bordered by Quincy, LaSalle, Clark, and Jackson stood the Grand Pacific Hotel. On October 11, 1883, sixty delegates representing the principal railways of North America met to standardize time. Up until this time each major city set its own time, often by means of a time ball—the last remaining example of such is the one used in Times Square to indicate midnight. Because of the Chicago convention, the midnight we see indicated in New York is not New York's real midnight but Philadelphia's midnight, as Eastern Standard Time is set at noon on the 75th meridian, the meridian that runs through Philadelphia, the headquarters of the Pennsylvania Railroad. The 90th meridian in Memphis, the 105th in Denver, the 120th in Fresno are the other noons we now live by. November 18, 1883, is the day known as the day of two noons when telegraphic signals were sent to reset all the local times and time became the time we think is time.

In the eleventh year of the war he writes: "The history of this period has also been written by the same Thucydides, an Athenian." Only a few sentences later

*Thucydides writes: "I lived through the whole of it being of an age to compre-
hend events and giving attention to them in order to know the exact truth
about them. It is also my fate to be an exile from my country for twenty years
after my command at Amphipolis."*

Platonic Harvests

In the back corner of the now old new wing of the Art Institute of Chicago
is the reconstructed Chicago Stock Exchange Trading Room designed by
Louis H. Sullivan in 1893. The elaborate stenciled applications, art glass
treatments, and molded plaster capitals were preserved when the Stock
Exchange was demolished in 1972. The Art Institute was able to recreate
the room in 1976 using the original salvaged elements. In the corner of the
trading room, hard against the coffered quarter-sawn oak-paneled walls is
an empty table. When the exchange was active, displayed on this table were
several piles of grain—wheat, oats, corn, barley—as an illustration to the
traders on the floor. The puts and calls being exchanged, the bids being bid,
were connected to an actual thing, real cereal, a commodity that had not,
as yet, evolved to pure algebraic abstraction. These products were already
part of the communal imagination of the traders who traded future futures,
where real futures were already bargained for in a now already-residing,
unreal present. The vast, severely modern bay of pits that replaced Mr.
Sullivan's Beaux Art guildhall was built without such a display table. There,
even that slim reed of graphic connection snapped, the real real cornered
now only in the tangled snapping ganglia of the shouting brokers, the syn-
apses of their electronic devices mimicking memory.

*In Book Four, Thucydides narrates the action of General Thucydides at
Amphipolis, describing there his own defeat that precipitated his own exile.
He records objectively, dispassionately, the story of General Thucydides as he
rushes to defend the city against the Spartan army led by King Brasidas but
arrives too late, the fall of the city sparking a regional revolt against Athens.
He is ostracized. Had he won the battle, the history of the battle would have
been different, of course. Had he won the battle, the history of the battle would
never had been written.*

North by Northwest Is Not a Real Direction

Mistaken identity. Masquerade. Camouflage. You remember. George Kaplan played by Roger Thornhill played by Cary Grant arrives on the 20th Century Limited at LaSalle Street Station disguised as a Red Cap, assisted in his escape by Eve Kendell played by Eve Kendell played by Eva Marie Saint. He shaves in the station restroom using a miniature travel razor—the scene prefiguring the finale's scramble on the cliff faces of Mount Rushmore. *North by Northwest*'s original title was *The Man in Lincoln's Nose*. But now we are in Chicago and Roger Thornhill is sent by Eve Kendall to a cornfield in Indiana to meet his nonexistent double George Kaplan, or so he thinks. You remember the rest. He do-si-does instead with the deadly crop-duster, a pas de deux in the dusty, flat fields outside Prairie, Indiana. Of course the scene was shot near Bakersfield, California, which appears on film as more Indiana than Indiana, or an exaggerated Indiana, an amplified Indiana. In the film, the pretend Indiana pretending to be Indiana becomes Indiana. But more striking for our purposes is to realize that this famous scene makes no sense. What machinations to lure the victim out to a remote cornfield to be killed by an admittedly ungainly and inaccurate weapon system! If you think about it, how did Martin Landau, playing the evil Leonard, throw such an elaborate operation together on such short notice and with what cost-benefit analysis to guarantee the desired result? The assassins themselves seem confused on the deadliest delivery device. Propeller decapitation? Automatic weapon strafing? Actual crop-dust dusting? No, the famous scene is a lark, a tour de force, is in the movie as a complete out-of-whack whack, a lyric moment in spite of, to spite, the picture's narrative oomph. The scene is the movie's made-up movie. *North by Northwest*'s theme dwells on the slippery nature of reality—I am mad but North-Northwest. This crazed scene is the real movie's madness. It makes make-believe make believe.

The nineteenth year of the war. Thucydides, writing of the exhausted Athenian army's slaughter in the Assinarus river near Syracuse, is first to use the image of a river running red with blood. "The Peloponnesians came down and butchered them ... in the water which was thus immediately fouled but which they went on drinking just the same, mud and all, bloody as it was, most even fighting each other to have it." Perhaps he was not the first to write such a set piece, but his is the first to survive. The river of history inked from now on with blood.

It's Okay in Practice, but What about Theory

He's an undergrad upperclassman showing prospective students and their families the University of Chicago's Hyde Park campus. His group is near the field where once the Manhattan Project ignited the first chain-reacting atomic pile when one of the kids asks what the students here do for fun. This kid has been to Northwestern to tour as well, has there heard about the dance marathon and the rock that gets painted over and over again by students who protect the rock's topmost coat. The rock has its own website and rock cam. "A scavenger hunt," the tour guide tells his glassy-eyed crew, "We have a scavenger hunt each spring. Last spring," he says, "a dozen teams of students searched the campus for parts to construct an atomic reactor." He turns and takes a step or two leading them toward the Econ building and the abstract sculpture designed to cast, on May Day, a shadow of the hammer and sickle. Perfectly timed, he stops and turns back to his following. He says, "Two of them worked."

Ostrakons were potsherds, broken pottery Athenians used to vote for exile. One's name was scratched into the shard. The ballot cast. Thucydides. I imagine an ostrakon with his name on it on Thucydides's table, a paperweight, a souvenir, as he writes his history and his History.

A Bread Crumb Essay

Best American Essays 2005

1979

"What's an 'MLA?'" I asked. The person I was asking was William Baer, a graduate student poet in The Writing Seminars of Johns Hopkins University. He stood in my office doorway. I was nearing the end of the first semester of my year as a lecturer there. Bill, who was older than I though a year behind me in the program, had asked me, "Going to the MLA?" In 2013, Bill retired from the Creative Writing Department of the University of Evansville, where he had taught for nearly twenty-five years. "The MLA," he said, "is where you go to interview for creative writing jobs." I did not know then what an MLA was. I had no idea, then, that there was a way to get a job teaching creative writing. My teachers at The Writing Seminars had not mentioned it. The one piece of vocational advice had been from John Barth, who suggested I teach remedial English as he had done when starting out at Penn State. In the fall of 1979, I hadn't given the future much thought at all, had barely thought of 1980. Grammar, I thought, would be the end of the road.

The airliner is nearly empty. I am flying from Alabama to Indianapolis for this year's Great Lakes Bookseller's Association meeting on one of the first flights once they resumed after the attacks a week before. There must be four of us scattered around the main cabin. The grim attendants sit down with us, chat about anything but. We all had been searched—cars, luggage, self— three or four times before boarding. The only joke had been how the joke was on those not flying as this flight would be safest trip ever now that . . . The attendance at the conference would be down, everyone expected. The demographics already skewed by the disappearance of independent bookstores, the consolidations of the chains and distributors, Amazon. There were many more vendors now—exhibitors and authors with new books— than curious customers. I had a new book to peddle, *The Blue Guide to Indiana*, a fake travel guide, the joke being that no one, not even folks from Indiana, toured the state. Jonathan Franzen was there too. *The Corrections* had just been released. We sat together with a dozen other authors making a show of it in the signing room, signing copies of our books for the few buyers who did appear for the promotion but mainly for each other. The hit of the conference, however, was Lynn Sherr's *America the Beautiful*, about the song. Returning home, I waited at the hastily constructed checkpoints at the airport while the new security agents looked through all my signed complimentary books.

1992

I am having my first and only coffee ever—it is an espresso—at an outdoor café in Asheville, North Carolina, with Angela Barrett. My heart instantly chatters within its chassis behind the breastbone. She is amused and attends fully to the data emerging from this experimental trial. She is more of a scientist than a writer, though we are here in town to teach writing, not science, at Warren Wilson College's low-residency MFA program. We had been wondering how a writer, me, had survived this long without the elixir of coffee. What was a writer anyway? The greater culture seemed to be moving to clearly define the role through certification, an MFA degree and course of study, though neither one of us had the papers our students would soon possess. As I idle and thrum at high revs, pigeons circle the obelisk, dive-bomb the crumbs scattered on the adjoining plaza. We conclude that we are the last or maybe the first of an old order or a new phylum, the schooled writer, the writing school. We contemplate visiting the nearby Riverside Cemetery and searching for the grave of the writer O. Henry, his stone, we hear, covered with pennies. But I am wound so tight I am unable to move.

1986

I gave up tenure at Iowa State and moved to Boston to teach undergraduate creative writing at Harvard for five years. The position is not tenure track, which means I will travel through the next several years never really able to settle into Cambridge, walking dead. Theresa and I do strike up a friendship with David Rivard and his wife Michaela Sullivan, an in-house graphic designer for Houghton Mifflin. She shows us the new powerful Apple computer in her office and the tools onboard that allow her to create the covers and page layouts. She shows me the cover of a new annual series—*Best American Essays*—published under the Ticknor and Fields imprint in a boxed set with the established series of *Best American Stories*. She manipulates the mouse to fan an array of Pantone colors, saying that in subsequent years the publisher will run the spectrum.

1980

Though the Apple computer was invented in 1976, Apple the company goes public this year. The share price is $22.00. At the same time Steve Jobs is convinced, after seeing it first at Xerox, that a graphical user interface would be the design of all future computing. I am typing this now, in 2015, on a 2012 iMac running OS X 10.8.5 with graphics NVIDIA GeForce GT 640 MS 12 MB. The machine creates the illusion on the screen in front of me that I am mechanically typing this "this" on a white, eight-and-a-half by eleven piece of paper. I am still using the hobbled QWERTY keyboard designed purposely to slow my typing on the typewriter so as not to jam the keys.

The bulletin boards of the Johns Hopkins Homewood campus, like bulletin boards of most campuses, are scalloped with neatly typed sheets of paper, the lower edge fringed with tear-away tongues printed with contact phone numbers, advertising typing. Theses, dissertations, once accepted, are bound by the university and stored in the library. Their pages must be perfect. Correction fluids or tapes cannot be used, so if a mistake is found, it often means the retyping of the entire page and sometimes subsequent pages as the correction spills letters or words forward, confounding the previous spacing. I tell my students today about this arrangement, mention that I received my degree in one year or really in nine months of the two semesters, but really really in six months because the book of stories I wrote for my thesis had to be completed by February in time for it to be typed perfectly, its format reviewed and accepted by the graduate school. I want to include pictures too—two color reproductions of postcards depicting Fort Wayne. Color xerography was brand new, and, I thought, lovely, with its melted wax crayon colors. After much discussion, a special dispensation is granted and the thesis was received with pictures.

1979

Elizabeth Spires, a poet in my class at Johns Hopkins, receives an IBM Correcting Selectric II for her birthday. The machine was and still is the paragon of electric typewriters and serves as the transition to the "word processor" and computer-based platforms of the future, what with its binary programming and minute data storage that allows the machine to remember the mistake and type back over it with correction tape. I am using, and I still have, a Smith Corona typewriter to create the worksheets for my fiction seminar, the basket of keys (not the spinning-ball element of the Selectric) striking the stencil of the mimeograph sheet hard enough to record its negative in wax on the reverse. There is always the razor blade to correct. Rolling the page out, separating the stencil from the waxed backing, and shaving off the offending adhered type. Even then, I swear I could tell the difference of writing produced by one machine over that of another. The electric machines hum as you think. Their "touch" too is all different even as the arrangement of the letters remained the same.

1995

The day before pickup in Syracuse, I poke through the discarded trash piled on the curb of the streets in my neighborhood. I find many Smith Corona typewriter cases, portables mostly, but some standard desktops nestle in the grass. Smith Corona's last American factory in the Cortland suburb has just closed, the works shifting down to Mexico. I am using, then, a Macintosh LC with a page display I opted for instead of a new color horizontal screen. I have just hooked the machine up to the university's electronic mail and have begun receiving messages and memos at home by means of a dial-up modem. I can access the World Wide Web only from a machine in my office at school. Every house in Syracuse, it seems, had a typewriter, and everyone seems, overnight, not to need them anymore. What to do with the old machines? Take them to the curb. Over time, I bring a few of the carcasses home with me. Walking the streets looking through the heaps for a new model, a different color, a better box, I see a few others scavenging. I tell myself the surplus would be for parts if nothing else, unable to imagine writing without a typewriter in the uncertain future.

1984

I return to Johns Hopkins in 1984. I visit the current seminar class, give a reading. I ask my former teacher, John Barth, how things are going. In four short years the number of creative writing programs has grown from two dozen to over one hundred. I have been teaching at Iowa State University those four years, growing a graduate program, an MA, so as not to conflict with Iowa's MFA program down the road. In the last four years, Iowa State has hired four new writers—Steve Pett, Jane Smiley, David Milofsky, and Mary Swander—adding to a staff of five already there. "It is more and more difficult to attract students," Jack tells me. I ask him where they are going. "To Syracuse," he says, "to work with Raymond Carver and Tobias Wolff."

1984

I live in Story County, Iowa, teaching at Iowa State University. Theresa Pappas and I start a small press, Story County Books, and bring out our first edition, a one-story chapbook by Michael Wilkerson titled *Can This Story Be Saved?* We want to take advantage of this new technology, the Macintosh computer's desktop publishing. We do not want to do something finely printed like Allen Kornblum's Toothpaste Press over in Iowa City, but discover what the new machine could do. It would be several years before I owned a Mac. There are only a few on campus. We rent one at an early print store that has several, on Lincoln Way across from the university.

1989

I start work on a book called *Townships*, an anthology of essays attempting to define the Midwest. I have this crazy idea that the geography of the American Midwest is characterized by the telltale checkerboard pattern of its landscape generated by the township grid. I ask twenty-five Midwestern writers to write an essay about the township—the 6-by-6-square-mile jurisdiction Thomas Jefferson dreamed up to grid the entire country—in which the writer grew up. I had just read David Foster Wallace's *Girl with Curious Hair*, curious about the homage to John Barth and the story "Westward the Course of Empire Takes its Way." He was living in Boston, too, and I ask him if he would like to contribute. "Derivative Sport in Tornado Alley," his essay, comes with graphic depictions of the geometry of the subject—empty boxes, blacked-in squares, and elongated rectangles. In the essay, he takes my abstract idea of very concrete grid and literally literalizes it.

In Maine, we are playing Mafia. Jonathan Lethem leads us in this party game, teams of insiders and outsiders, the Mafia and the Innocents, through sustained periods of deception and discussion. The teams are made up of writers and participants of the Stonecoast Writers Conference, an evening's entertainment after the nightly reading. I met Jonathan the year before. He visited the University of Alabama to do a reading. Afterward, we played Mafia. This was at Andy and Sydney Duncan's house, writers who had met Jonathan years before at an independent workshop in North Carolina, interested in transgressive forms, bending genre.

There is a great unease with the complicated communities the great sorting engine of the university tolerates. Writers, I think, think of themselves sometimes as individual agents, unique, original but at the same time long for inclusion, connection. Jonathan moves in circles that occasionally touch or intersect the interlocking rings of the university, the maturing genre of a writing program. In the game, there is "night" and "day."

I am invited to be a visiting professor at The Ohio State University. It is called a "sprint semester," a week of classes on any subject, and I choose "collage." I choose collage, a non-narrative form, just to push back a bit against the bias of realistic narrative that has dominated prose workshops in the twenty years I have been teaching. John Gardner's *The Art of Fiction*, published in 1983, had been wired into workshops and emphasized transparency and unselfconscious storytelling. This aesthetic insists that a text not call attention to itself, that it create a sustained dream. Its conventions are clear and teachable as craft, and its message coincides with the rapid and vast expansion of writing programs. Ironically, the principle of transparency becomes enforced at the very moment that the machine writers use to compose their writing becomes expansive and expressive. Writers in workshops are encouraged to rig their powerful typesetting machines, now connected to the Internet, to produce finished copy that looks exactly like the product of an early twentieth century typewriter. E. J. Levy is in the class, composing prose from prompts of paint sample strips, photo booth photos, and other graphic interruptions. The time is ripe. The writers in that sprint semester class have all grown up with the computer, with cable TV and remote control. They are comfortable with the lyric and the non-narrative, with comic books and video games.

The Best American Essays 2005 is an anniversary issue, the twentieth, and the series editor, Robert Atwan, looks backward to the book's inception in 1986. I consider my contribution, "Contributor's Note," the only time I have ever appeared, to be a fictive essay. I was surprised that it was considered. The piece, in the form of a contributor's note, traces the biography of a "Michael Martone" and his life performing public readings of his own work or attending similar literary readings by others in the vast network of creative writing programs and conferences that have emerged in the preceding twenty years. As the piece of writing attempts to defamiliarize the author's note, the whole volume makes me re-see the history of creative writing program culture. My whole life turns strange for me. In order for a life to have meaning, one must get outside of that life to see what matters in all the stuff that happened. The memoirist, I think, often draws a closed parenthesis, simulates a death, so that the time before can begin making a sense. Think my junior year abroad. Think my childhood. The book for me draws such a parenthesis. I can look back over the cultural shifts and aesthetic arguments I lived through and survived. The 2005 edition also balances on an edge of another era, marking, perhaps, the moment the essay was changing. In what way would the essay and its practitioners enter into an academic setting as the new discipline there—"creative nonfiction." The inclusion of my "essay" makes me look back in another way. It was originally published in *Flyway*, a journal still published at Iowa State University and one I edited in the early eighties when it was known as *Poet & Critic*. It was my first job right after graduate school. I inherited a format from an even earlier time. Poets who had pieces accepted for the magazine were given other poems also to be published there. They were then to write a round robin of critiques that would be printed on the pages facing the poems, a workshop in print. But even by 1980 this device had no novelty left in it, and almost every contributing poet had already done time in a workshop for real. I changed the format. I thought then, and think now, that 1980 marked the complete naturalization of "the workshop" for American poets. Fiction writers would not be that far behind. Twenty-five years later, I find the essays in this volume poised on a similar threshold of the schoolhouse door and the workshop seat at the very same moment that academic programs begin once more to entertain other forms of prose besides that of the narrative and the realistic.

Saving the Daylights out of Saving Daylight

Once, one fall, in the middle of the night, I was riding the Broadway Limited west from New York to Fort Wayne when the train came to a squeaking, creaking halt in the middle of an Ohio cornfield. Such delays are not all that unusual on Amtrak, which runs its routes over private rails. Passenger trains are often shunted off to a siding to let the proprietor freight have the right-of-way. But this pause was different. The country's time was falling back; time zone after time zone time was turning back time. This wrought havoc with the train's schedule. If we hadn't stopped, we'd actually arrive early at the next station. We had to let the schedule catch up. I stood looking out the open top of the Dutch door in the vestibule between cars. Cornfields everywhere. All over the country, trains waited, panting, stopped in their tracks. Out of time, I waited for the hour to overtake us all, slamming by us, expedited, a true "Limited"—tracks cleared, high-balling west.

more

Michael Downing in his remarkable book *Spring Forward* mentions this phenomenon of stalled trains along with many other skewed consequences, strange and stranger, of what he calls *Spring Forward: The Annual Madness of Daylight Saving Time*. It is an admirable popular history of this intriguing mass hysteria in a class with Michael Pollan's deciphering the tulip madness in his book *The Botany of Desire* or Marvin Harris's materialist decoding of the potlatch in *Cows, Pigs, Wars, and Witches*. Not quite a *Wisconsin Death Trip*, *Spring Forward* does, however, shake its head at the long, strange journey "time" has taken and the strange manifestation of its manifestation of both its pastness and its futureness—not simply figuratively but quite literally, a persistent residue and befuddled ritual, in our apparently adjustable present present midst.

more

On another train, at another time. It was New Year's and I was heading west. The coach I rode roused itself on *a* midnight to sing "Auld Lang Syne," a synchronized celebration with the ball dropping in Times Square, the terminus from which we had departed. There was improvised confetti, pitiful horns, splits of champagne, opportunistic kissing. We chugged through the night, crossing, in the dark, some line of demarcation. Now in Indiana we resumed our initial places, wound backward to wait for the year to end again, start again. There was another countdown. The singing started up on cue—the engine's Dopplered horn yodeling. The confetti defied gravity. The bubbles found their way back into the champagne. Brand new kisses were minted out of the ones recently scrapped.

more

The drama of *Spring Forward* is between the notion of time connected to the motion of the planet and the various machines and schemes that regulate it in theory. It is the disconnection of the first from the second that Mr. Downing stages here with great precision. He is particularly adept at constructing the narrative of this conflict found in the arguments of government hearing rooms and the daily decaying *news* of newspapers. All of these embedded stories always boil down to the same conclusion. The more Daylight Saving Time is studied the more confusing it becomes to its students. The contemplation of time seems to infect everyone with this special malaise. All seem helpless, hapless before the inevitability of this idea whose time has, well, come and keeps coming.

more

The book, of course, is also trapped in a kind of time. That is to say any book has an existential imperative of beginning, middle, and end, and this book flows that way starting at the beginning and moving through its time as if on rails. It was the railroads (having unleashed a machine that, in fact, traveled faster than time) that standardized time in the first place. This is, of course, covered here. There is a plaque affixed to the side of the building in Chicago—the site where time was, well, fixed, where, by fiat, time was fitted out as another Midnight Special, its own locomotive. No accident, then, that Einstein himself dispatched an animated example of an engine to tame the wild notions of relativity. This book, but not just this book, is stuck in its own irresistible progressions of time, its free-floating forwardness. Forward! Perhaps backward. But rarely repetitious and never simultaneous. One word after the other. Alas, our time-honored timely timed madness wired, now, into us.

more

Once, one fall, in the middle of the night, I was riding the Broadway Limited west from New York to Fort Wayne when the train came to a squeaking, creaking halt in the middle of an Ohio cornfield. Such delays are not all that unusual on Amtrak, which runs its routes over private rails. Passenger trains are often shunted off to a siding to let the proprietor freight have the right-of-way. But this pause was different. The country's time was falling back; time zone after time zone time was turning back time. This wrought havoc with the train's schedule. If we hadn't stopped, we'd actually arrive early at the next station. We had to let the schedule catch up. I stood looking out the open top of the Dutch door in the vestibule between cars. Cornfields everywhere. All over the country, trains waited, panting, stopped in their tracks. Out of time, I waited for the hour to overtake us all, slamming by us, expedited, a true "Limited"—tracks cleared, high-balling west.

more

Time in a Vacuum Bottle

A Genealogy

My father worked as a telephone switchman. He tended the old mechani-cal switches in hot, windowless switch rooms back when all the telephones were still dial telephones. The switches clicked and stuttered as someone somewhere dialed a number. The noise the dialing made was not distracting enough to keep him awake. He drank black coffee black. The box that held the mechanism for the current time and temperature number had a little porthole. He watched the reels of tape, spooling and unspooling through the night, inside the building that sighed and chirped all around him.

At the city's filtration plant, Uncle Rick sat behind a desk and gauged the dials, opening and closing the valves by hand, filed reports, took samples. The water seeped by design. It rose slowly up through the layers of sand, shedding the floc. The water welled up, skinned off the percolating pool in clean clean sheets. The plant was vast. A local college used the huge limestone building in its advertisements. It looked more like a college than the college. At night he nursed coffee laced with rum.

My great-uncle Ward walked the catwalks through the wavy updrafts of heat above the boilers. The powerhouse where he worked nights sang, the dynamos in close harmony with each other backed by the brush snare of live steam. On weekends, he played clarinet in a Dixieland band; during the week, he practiced in the yawning room. The big loft windows reached up, opened, three stories tall, with all the stars mapped out in the panes' grid. He drank hot tea he mixed with cold milk, kept an eye on the auger worming coal from the bunker into that constant fire.

My mother's brother, Uncle Wayne, worked summers and school vacations at a meatpacker. He cleaned, with high-pressure steam, the stainless steel vats where the chopped scraps of meat were processed, kneaded into stuffing casings for franks, baloneys, loafs. In a jumpsuit and hair net, his shoes wrapped like cuts of meat, he slid to the bottom of the metal bowl through the scummy fat left behind after the mix had been extruded. At school he studied radiation, diagnostic, not therapeutic, turned flesh invisible. He ate peanut butter sandwiches for lunch at midnight. No cold cuts. The coke he drank still had the little leftover lozenges of ice he'd grind into nothing with his back teeth.

My father's father was a janitor at the Hotel Indiana. He worked nights snaking drains in unoccupied rooms, spackling walls, then sanding and painting, changing the long tubes of florescent lights. He had a room in the basement where he sat through the night, waiting for a call from the front desk, sorted work orders by the light of a naked bulb. He drank soup early in the morning just before the guests began to stir in the rooms upstairs, washed it down with coffee. He swept. He swept a lot. The crushed cigarette butts on the terrazzo floor of the grand lobby and the marble steps up to the mezzanine. One night, moving furniture, he was blinded in his one good eye (the other already cloudy with cataracts) when a spring sprung, exploding through the cushion of a couch he had just leaned over and begun to lift.

My cousin Anthony owned a tent rental business. Early in the mornings or late at night he would set up his tents or take them down. He had a crew, but he often worked alone. At dawn dew collected on the grass, or it was frost. He also managed dozens of coin-operated Bingo machines he moved between VFW posts, fraternal lodges, and church basement halls. He never took a break. His Thermos, empty, rolled back and forth on the floorboard of his truck.

My other grandfather read meters during the day, walking house to house, but several nights a week he worked at a full-service filling station downtown across from the newspaper building. He closed up after midnight, after the newsroom editors and reporters called it a day. It was a Standard Oil shop, a white tiled box with blue trim, two bays and two pumps. Hoses crisscrossed the driveways. Cars running over them triggered the loud bell over the door. He spooned up a late supper, stale bread and cinnamon sugar soaked in cold milk, between the trips out to the pumps to pump the gas, check the oil, check the air, wiping his hand often on a rag he yanked from his back pocket.

Uncle Forest, my grandmother's brother, was the projectionist at the Embassy downtown. An old theater, it was built before safety stock film, when they still used open flame. The booth was attached like a balcony to the façade of the building, a blister high up on the outside of the theater, perched there delicately. If it happened to catch fire, the whole room could be cut away, slide down the side of the building on fire, isolating the flames from the great hall inside. Forest, in the dark, smoked and sipped coffee, the light from below sifting up through the old warping floorboards illuminating the clouds of smoke from his cigarettes.

Thermostat

I touch it every day, a secular mezuzah at the threshold of climatic change. On the wall, at eye level, a floor above the furnace it regulates, it is connected and remote. A hemispheric sconce embossed with the proprietary brand on its clear bubble: HONEYWELL. With the tread of my fingertip, I nudge the clear cleats of the inner ring delicately, dialing a safe, toward the triggering calibration of the two fine red needles, one below indicating, its shadow falling upon the numbered scale, how it feels and the other, on top, quivering as it inches toward the desired state.

Henry Dreyfus designed it, just another mechanical object in the stream of streamlining. Modern to imagine everything smoothed, rounded, shaped by a constant manipulation. The wearing away. Friction as artist. All this metal in our hands pliant, malleable, plastic even, warmed to the touch, to the point of melting, molded into these organic solids of French curves so that even the most inanimate of things looked (when not moving) to move. Everything designed for speed, molting molecule by molecule, thin peelings of skin, a response to the constant abrasion of invisibly moving air. The rubbing away. The erasure to the point of sculpted, cupped parentheses. Perfectly still but still in motion.

Thermostat. Heat, of course, but in "stat" cleaves both the sense of immediate, the "stat" of televised code blues, and the "stat" of passive regulation. Stationary. Statistics. Standstill. The instrument for feedback. As is skin. A touch. A response to touch. The shiver. The twitch. The gooseflesh. The blush. Mine is anodized. Beneath the cowling, the mechanism of static. The watch spring and the bulb of quaking quicksilver that trembles on its mirrored surface, responding to the eddies of my breath and, when I stop breathing, to the reverb of my heart transmitted through the cold air.

I touch it, and touching it I ease the imagined temperature past the ambient one. At that moment, deep in the house, I feel that sound like the distant launching of mortars, an inhalation of air as the oxygen in the room around me is drawn down the returns, the jets of blue flame igniting somewhere.

The Zoo We Thought We Bought Bought Us

How the Shape of Shape Shapes Us

In 1978, the Seattle architectural firm of Jones and Jones published their revolutionary work, *Gorilla Habitat, Comprehensive Plan, Woodland Park Zoo*. The plan, based on "landscape immersion," sought to construct a zoo that was not a zoo, disguising the apparatus of captivity and confusing artfully the distinction between the animal on view and the one doing the viewing. Ten years later in an *Atlantic* article, Melissa Greene refers to a letter sent by Dian Fossey, the famed primatologist and consultant on the project, who had shown photographs of the Seattle exhibit to her colleagues at the scientific station in Rwanda, reporting that they were convinced the photos of gorillas at the zoo were taken in the wild. Fossey, as a consultant, had flown to Washington state. Driving in from the airport, David Hancocks, the principle of the project, recalls they were anxious to get from her a sense of what the Rwandan highland rainforest looked like. Fossey, pointing out the car's windows, said, "It looks like that! It looks just like that!" The designers learned from that encounter that they could stop "designing" and let the native plants go native, be invasive, naturalizing the exhibit. And they did.

Brothers and sisters, my text today is not drawn from the books of Bakhtin or Shklovsky. Instead, let's open our missals to the verses of St. Thomas Kuhn and *The Structures of Scientific Revolutions*. Kuhn argued that science progressed through a series of paradigm shifts, not in a continuous linear fashion. Once the paradigm of physics, say, is in place, he argued, science busies itself mainly with "mopping up" the details of the phenomenon the paradigm defines. Individual experiments never overthrow the paradigm but reaffirm the paradigm's initial elegance and predictive nature. That is to say, most of science isn't so much about discovering new knowledge as it is about corroborating and collaborating with the paradigm. Scientists hate Kuhn, as he depicts most of what they do as not original but custodial. Scientists get testy when pictured merely testing the veracity of the paradigm, not testing the phenomenon itself.

Many of us write our books in or near, cheek to jowl with, university and college labs. To what extent do we labor in the structuring of our books—let's call them novels—in a paradigmatic way, or do we work in the form as a received and clearly defined paradigm? Are we when we write a novel, even a novel that experiments with such elements as relativistic point of view, time, tense, transparency or self-consciousness, "mopping-up"? The formal innovations we seek to introduce might be seen from the remove of the paradigm as mere tweaks to the structure. This behemoth superstructure absorbs the tinkering as part of the already fabricated form that is defined as "Novel." This Novel overstories our mere understorying stories. Like our scientific colleagues, we labor in the belief our efforts are original when they are, in fact, fully expected and anticipated. The cultural expectations are for the writer to be mainly curatorial, to contribute to the Novel paradigm, the tradition of the novel. The real action of innovative shape-changing is not within the genre but at the level of genre. We think we are the keepers of the zoo that houses the novel when in fact we might be kept by the zoo that is the novel.

For example. I can say I wrote this paper, that I am the originator of this paper, and in writing a paper about other shapes the writer of a novel might deploy beyond the narrative, I, the writer of this paper, thought I would incorporate structural disruptions and participatory flourishes into the text's flow to demonstrate alternative means of structuring "a paper," extrapolating such formal innovations into the target novel form.

I can say I wrote this paper, but to what extent can we all say that the conference steering committee of AWP "wrote" this paper? Or more exactly, to what extent can we say that they structured the form of the paper, a matrix, if you will, a lath onto which I trowel a text? To what extent was this paper written already for me by the AWP?

I wrote this paper, but to what extent can I say that the management and employees of the Hilton Hotel Company who have constructed the fixed form of the delivery device of said paper wrote it? To what extent was the form of my paper and its delivery dictated, not by me, but by the building codes of the municipality of the City of Chicago enforced by the attentive eye of its fire marshal?

In *Thor Power Tool Company v. Commissioner*, 439 U.S. 522 (1979), the United States Supreme Court upheld IRS regulations limiting how taxpayers could write down inventory and in so doing rewrote the form of the American novel. Prior to the Thor decision a publisher's backlist was its most valuable asset. Once that inventory could not be written down, a publisher's frontlist was its only asset, forcing the need to produce instantly profitable block-busters that justified the expense of warehousing. Publishers could no long afford to sell a few hundred copies of a "good" book a year, year after year. Such books were pulped or sold into the remainder market. A consequence of this 1979 decision, the year I graduated a master in literary fiction, was the rise of Barnes & Noble, whose business specialized in selling remaindered books. In Thor, the court existentially changed the nature of publishing's business model, and in an interesting coincidence, corresponded to a cultural and artistically critical discussion of the death of the novel. The novel survived, of course, by seeking refuge in nonprofit publishing enterprises or by becoming commercially viable in the new business environment. The individual writers of novels may believe that the series of aesthetic choices they make is theirs to make, but those choices are influenced subtly and not so subtly by these larger nonartistic structures and strictures, conglomerations of economic and political forces that force the writer to adapt or cloister. That cloistering comes, of course, with its own stints, constraints, and demands—think tenure and patronage policies. We may arrange the spaces inside these cages, our offices, our departments. Look, the dappled light spilling through the barred and shuttered windows casts a dappled shadow on the pages on which we write. Film noir was not the original invention of the auteur of the genre but a structured response to the imposition of the Hayes Office's censorship codes.

The structure for this paper was predetermined. One of its strictures was that it be fifteen minutes in length. Fifteen minutes in length to accommodate four papers, introductions of their authors, and time for questions. I choose to burn now one of my fifteen minutes with one minute of silence. Timekeeper.

Hey! What a good-looking audience! Anybody from the University of Alaska, Fairbanks! I spent a week there once as a visiting writer and wrote in what was a profoundly different cultural and material substrate generating fictive narrative. Forget for a minute monstrous vegetables grown in the college gardens. Forget for a minute the young Japanese couples who visit to copulate, it is believed fortuitously, beneath the Northern Lights. Forget for a minute that light to dark ratio does not vary day to day by minutes but by quarter hours. Forget for a minute that writers live in cabins with no running water, as buried pipes would melt the tundra. Forget for a minute that writers are propelled by means of dog-powered skijoring and that room is made in each classroom for said dogs to relax and roughhouse together before the journey to the next class. All strange indeed. But consider what the journeyman writers of the University of Alaska, Fairbanks, attend to for their RA stipend. That is really strange. Manning camouflaged huts on the four corners of a vast enclosure they observe the musky sex lives of the musk ox, a procedure described to me as the determined mounting of one haystack onto another. I imagine the love stories generated by the close and endless observation of such ground-hugging clouds, the plodding plotting on the gridded maps of space, the rendezvous of a prehistoric species brought back from the brink of extinction to infect our own cowed dreams.

"'Well, clear this out now!' said the overseer, and they buried the hunger artist, straw and all. Into the cage they put a young panther. Even the most insensitive felt it refreshing to see this wild creature leaping around the cage that had so long been dreary. The panther was all right. The food he liked was brought to him without hesitation by the attendants; he seemed not even to miss his freedom . . ."

To the caged animal the cage is just the cage. It is by definition nonmalleable, immutable, irresistible, static. Artists in the cage, we bend, we change, we adapt to the discipline of the cage, do not miss our freedom as much as welcome the confining definition of the structures we inhabit. When the cage is just a cage it is perfectly disguised as a cage. It is the embodiment of off-limits limits. We have room to frolic, to bound in our bounded precincts. We look through the bars to see the other animals seemingly enmeshed in their own cages. We look and they look, but both of us, caught up in our cages of seeing, see no other way to see.

Some Space

1.

A month ago I was tying a red-polka-dotted pink ribbon and white satin bow to the trunk of a cherry tree. The viewing of the cherry blossoms, *sakura*, was waning, the petals left on the bloom ragged, muscled aside by the surging green leaves, the sublime and melancholy image of a fall in the spring.

The orchard is in a field at the crook where the interstate stub branches into the one-way arteries of Lurleen Wallace Boulevard, circulating into the heart of downtown Tuscaloosa.

We have a sister city, Narashino, in Japan, recovering, then and now, from the tsunami, the earthquake. The ribbons are a token, a kind of meditation on our fragile, distant connection.

Organized quickly, the group, a handful of volunteers, fanned out through the orchard. Our arms cradled the notions. It looked as if we were attempting to reattach bouquets of petals to the blown trees.

There is this orchard here, foiled by the back of the Goodyear garage. Another on the campus overlooks the stadium plaza and its huddle of statues of champion football coaches. A third, a massive display, is planted out by the JVC plant on the east side of the city and may be contemplated by the distracted passengers of cars rushing by on the interstate. In bloom, that orchard is a brilliant cumulus cloud, a smear of smoke near the ground.

Our task complete, there were pictures to be taken, posed before the bedecked trees. Cars, trucks on either side zoomed. We stood still, better to be captured still. Around us a light breeze lifted the shimmering spotted ribbons, a kind of sigh. The air plucked more petals from the blossoms and spun them around and around. Our friends in Japan reported back to us that in the wreck of tsunami they had found a few cherry blossoms to regard.

Posed, we gazed off into that distance beyond the photographer, assessed the perspective, the cleaved road coming together pointing south. Yesterday, a month later, the tornado stepped over that highway, there, just at the vanishing point, and wedged its way into the city.

2.

The school where I teach advertises itself as The University of Alabama—
Touching Lives. The televised graphic is a pulse generated in a classroom,
an expanding circle ever widening as the camera pulls out farther and farther even into outer space, that ripple, that wave emanating from little ol'
Tuscaloosa, there below, a speck of dirt on the moldy map of earth.

Teaching my students haiku, I have them consider the architecture of contrast. A minute gesture juxtaposed against the infinite. I take them out to
Marrs Spring, the water source the college grew up around beginning in
the 1830s. We watch frogs jump into the old pond, see the ripples ripple outward. Each composes a verse on the spot, use cell phones, text the poem to
a friend, a relative. I remind them that we live now in this electromagnetic
soup—text, data, digital dots and dashes emanating invisibly all around
us until we draw them back out of the congested air. A few telling words.
"Where are you now?"

They send their poems out into the world. We wait, contemplate the still
water. Then their devices, a chorus, suddenly animate in their hands, begin
to vibrate and croak, announcing, reverberating, the responses. From near.
From far.

Last night, I had a little power at my house as the darkness settled over
us all. I sent out pulses into space. My students, scattered by the storm,
still clutched that rapidly diminishing charge in their hands. Their phones
retained some spark. They echoed back. Outside, the thick air—still sultry,
saturated, heavy—transmitted the sawing of actual frogs in nearby gullies
and sloughs. "Here." And "here." And "here." The box in my palm peeped.
Spent, ratcheted down, one by one, the tiny tinny flashes fewer and fewer
as the batteries elsewhere everywhere died. There and there and there. And,
then, all that nothing.

3.

In Tuscaloosa, there is a woman, a neighbor, who walks every day from one side of town to the other, west to east to west. As she walks, she rants and preaches, cannot be persuaded to stop, cannot be talked to. She walks.

There was plenty of warning yesterday. Sirens. I raced home from campus, west by car into the rain wall, distant, the approaching storm working its way up the Black Warrior River.

Just blocks from both our homes, I catch up with the woman who walks, not walking, standing in the empty space on the corner of MLK and 6th. The space, there, is fallow, an open field, a ruin, still, of the 1840 tornado that cleared Newtown, Alabama, from the map. A nearby plaque attests to that disaster. The woman spreads open the folds of her poncho. Sails unfurling in the mounting wind, the cape whipping all around her. Then, her head down, into the wind, she walks the rest of the way home.

Asymmetry

>

I could actually close my eye. I
had to think about it. Think, "Blink!"
to blink. But it wasn't so much a
blink. It was more like weightlifting,
locating the muscle of the lid and
then sustained concentration,
feeling as if I were hauling down
an overhead garage door through
muscled telepathy. No, it was more
hydraulic, the fluid replaced by a
fluid energy that I forced, via my
mind, to flow. The lid slid down.
Not so much a blink though but an
elaborately constructed squint—a
wreck of creased skin, debris of
lashes, twitching. I closed my eye. I
think I thought I couldn't feel it. I
had to go see it for myself.

>

I think there are a dozen cranial
nerves. VII is the facial nerve that
provides the underlying architecture
of animation, of expression. Two
branches crisscross out of the brain,
tickle the ears threading beneath
the lobe, and then fan into the
face to message the underlying
muscle. These nerves are not about
transmitting feeling. Afflicted, I
could still feel my face and my face

could feel. Hot, cold, pain, pleasure.
No, the nerves there are about
transmitting feeling, not to the
brain, but broadcasting outward,
staging muscle into the semaphore
of expression, the wigwag of how we
feel, not what we are feeling.

>

It is more than a little bit creepy
to think of the entities that dwell in
the nerve fabric that knits up our
own thinking, the viruses latent there
below, inside. Chicken pox nesting
in the ganglia since the childhood
infection and outbreak, cracking
open and hauling itself, hand-over-
hand along the strand of the nerve
to the skin there to express itself as
shingles. Rashes, cold sores, lesions.
My face afflicted was featureless and
smooth. Ironed, wrinkle-free. Not
the usual M.O. of a virus, the telltale
trail of cell death. But, perhaps, they
think, a virus creeps, sleepwalks
along the sheath, makes it swell, fail.
Antiviral agents do nothing to the
nothing that is the palsy. A latent
virus might short the nerve or, for all
they think, it might not.

>

The famous map of narrative
is cock-eyed. It's not the isosceles
triangle we imagine we imagine.
The beginning, middle, and end.
Like the heft of letters in the phrase
"beginning, middle, and end,"
narrative is asymmetrical, skewed,

shrinking as it expands after the
spike, a sloping away. The sighing
denouement. Not a mountain in
cross-section as much as the gesture
of a drift, the sheer face of the cliff all
eroded on the lee side of the climax.
The upside down checkmark trails
off . . .

>

It started with a smacking of my
lips. I smacked my lips. I have a bowl
of yogurt at night, most every night,
a dessert, watching *The Daily Show*.
I use a spoon, an old Northwest
Airlines flatware spoon. And that
night spooning the yogurt into my
mouth, squeegeed off the spoon by
my lips, I half-heard the smack. I
couldn't have made the sound. Odd, I
half-thought.

>

Bell's palsy is diagnosed by
excluding other causes the paralysis
mimics—tumors, diabetes, Lyme
disease, asymptomatic herpes zoster,
head trauma, stroke, especially
stroke. Stroke because it shares with
Bell's the rapidity of the attack and its
handedness. But in the differential,
a stroke blacks out a sizeable side
of the body's real estate, while Bell's
blanks only one side of the face. Bell's
is, then, what it's not. Idiopathic.
Cryptogenic.

>

That night, I brushed my teeth.
I tried to spit in the sink. The spit,
instead of streaming toward the
drain, vectored to the right and
welled on the left, leaking out
there in that corner of my mouth.
Spitting, I had never given it a
second thought. It seemed to be

something one just does effortlessly, unconsciously, until one is made conscious of it. I brush with my right hand. My hair is parted on the left. I don't look in the mirror as I brush my teeth but look down into the ovoid stainless bowl. I put the brush down, turned the right (facing me) handle "on." Cold water. And cupped my right hand to catch a palm full of water, already spilling out of my hand, and brought it to my mouth. My ability to create suction was off too, much of the water fell back to the sink, the rest sloshing right, seeping already as I leaned back down to spit. I couldn't purse my lips. A fan of spit with elevated levels of undiluted toothpaste pasted the high, drier sides of the bowl. Odd, I thought again.

>

Dr. Sally Bell Beck sat me down and told me I was not insane. This was years ago. I was a freshman at Butler University, taking her introduction to psychology class. She told me she had this talk with many freshmen who, upon learning that one definition of madness was for the one who is mad not to know one is mad, thought oneself mad. You are not mad, she said, wiping at her right eye. But how can I tell, I asked her, if the symptom of my madness is that I don't know I am mad. Dr. Sally Bell Beck sighed, gave me her famous fish eye stare. The right half of her face, the sinister side facing her, was frozen. The skin there pulled taut, ironed. She was afflicted with some kind of permanent palsy that must have been with her since she was a student in college. In class, I would close my right eye, hold the textbook up to mask her face in half in class as she lectured, blotting out the still animated side. The half that didn't move appeared to be that of a youth, an ingénue, airbrushed. She talked out of the other side of her mouth, a kind of pirate's bark. And she always carried a massive handkerchief to dab at her walleye. To blink, she rolled her head down, tucking her chin to her chest, every minute or so. Then she rolled her staring eye up under the passive lid. It reappeared, glossy, as her head rolled back up, pointing her chin to the ceiling. The tears collected on the lip of the lower lid, spilled onto that smooth cheek she would dab away with the handkerchief. The lecture she gave each year on the psychology of love was famous at the school and was always attended by former students, staff, and faculty. Each fall, word got around campus that this was the week for the love lecture. I went years after I was her student, crowded into the classroom where most of the auditors stood staring at Dr. Sally Bell Beck nodding and tearing as she talked.

>

"Crocodile tears" are thought to be
synthetic sympathy, manufactured
grief. The nerve now off-line
producing the Bell's palsy in the
muscles of my face also worms its
way into the anterior two-thirds
of my tongue. I was warned that,
as the nerve rebooted, I might find
myself crying at the taste and/
or smell of food, a syndrome of
crocodile tears. I might also salivate
when I cried, but though the crossed
wiring had a certain symmetry, the
latter manifestation would be less
noticeable, a minor key, distracted
as I would be by the true sadness
generating the authentic tears.

>

I enjoy the television series *House*.
I watch the detective diagnostician
drama in reruns while eating yogurt.
I might have even been watching
House the night the palsy struck.
At my doctor's, I laughed, finding
out that the measurement of my

paralysis would be determined by
the House Brackman Facial Nerve
Grading System. The laugh spilled
out of one side of my malfunctioning
mouth, a characteristic of grade IV,
moderately severe, function. I smiled
my broken smile. It tickled as he
measured "the lateral movement of
the oral commissure."

>

I didn't think twice about the
anomalies of the night before. The
smacking of lips. The spraying of
spit. The next day I held conferences
all day in the student center. I staked
out a table near the Starbuck's
concession, where I can purchase
an Izze tangerine-flavored soda in a
bottle I will nurse through the dozen
half-hour meetings with students. I
sat across the table from one, looking
into his or her face as we talked, a
kind of mirror, about rising action
and falling action, the nature of fact

and fiction, the depth and surface
of character. As the day wore on I
felt stranger and stranger. I noticed
while drinking from the pop bottle
that I couldn't form a seal around
the opening. I could feel a weakness
in my face growing weaker. I began
to touch my face, knead the skin. It
felt a little like a dentist's block, like it
should be numb and with a phantom
puffiness as if severely swollen. But
when I actually touched my lips, they
felt normal, and, even more strangely,
I could feel via my lips, my fingers
touching there. I wasn't anesthetized,
yet I wasn't all there.

>

Had the attack been worse and I
had lost the ability to blink my left
eye, I would have been prescribed
an eye patch to protect it, to keep it
from drying out. Instead, I seemed
to weep, the tears welling out of my
eye and running down my cheek.

With effort I could close my eye,
blink away the tears. The attack had
come on overnight and disappeared
as quickly three weeks later. No
eye patch. But no more wearing
of contact lenses in order to avoid
scratching the dehydrated cornea.
The doctor had prescribed drops,
artificial tears, to be administered
before sleep just in case. Lying down,
I stared up toward the dropper,
saw a drop suspended there, saw
it fall, saw it accelerate toward my
eye. My brain sent signals, I know.
Automatic messages were posted
to protect the eye, but the lid didn't
budge. The artificial tears splashed
on my eye, the unblinking eye.
There was a chance I slept then with
one eye open. But after the drop I
shimmied the eyelid closed through
a concentrated effort. And once it
was closed it stayed closed. It would
be too hard to open. It patched itself.
It stayed closed until the elaborate
effort I had to muster the next
morning to prop the lid open again.

>

At first, I thought it was the
right side of my face that had gone
haywire when it had been the left.
The doctor was on the phone. I had
called him from the conferences in
the student center. He asked which
side of my face was affected. I had
the phone pressed against my right
ear. The right, I said. I had just forced
myself to smile. The right side of the

face snapped to attention, the smile
wedging the cheek into the hand
clutching the phone. The right, I said.
But, I think now, I thought it was the
right initially because the movement
there felt unnatural, the test gesture
was self-conscious, and, in the
absence of the other half of the
face, the sneering fragment of smile
seemed twitchy, a spasm, out of my
control. In contrast, the deadpan left
side seemed polite and understated
in its demeanor, seemed cautiously
detached from what felt like a manic
neighbor, all slapstick and pratfalls,
demonstrating its dexterity, its
benign innervation.

>

Tying ties in the mirror. Ties
untied are asymmetrical. The wide
and the narrow. The long end and the
short end draped around the neck,
worked to the suitable off-balanced,
out-of-kilter starting position. As I

knotted my ties, I would mug into the mirror exaggerated grimaces, leers, sneers. Mined, mimed my mien. I aped aspect. But still half my face was dumb to the body language bouncing off the mirror. I couldn't raise a reaction in half of me that couldn't act. It was as if I were looking askance at my own death mask, that masquerade. The stalled side of my face was lifelike, waxy, true to life but lifeless. Affectless. Bored. There it was in deep in the depth of the mirror, elsewhere.

>

Let's get the stroke business out of the way right now. Talking to the doctor on the phone from the conference table in the coffee shop, I asked if this was a stroke. Could I move my arms? Could I hear? See? Were my legs numb? Could I speak? Yes, I said, yes to all of that. Except my legs. My legs weren't numb. Or, more exactly, hissed. I lisped though the bilabial consonants. I lost the *b* sound and the *p*. The lips on the one side of the face had opted out of the phonics, had sent in a kind of nasally inflected *m*, a mushy plosive, the air let out of the tire, a flat *b*. The lips on the port side had been mashed, felt swelled. Not a stroke with its serious erasures. This something else with its awkward muscle amnesia. Its bumbled mumbling. This profiled scourge. This vacant duplex, gone fishing face.

>

Soon after the paralysis settled in,
I took my doughy face to a student
reading. I was still getting used to
my condition. Should I drink from
the bottle of water picked up from
the refreshment table? Teaching, I
am on the side that believes that the
best strategy is to call attention to an
anomaly before the students notice,
get ahead of the distraction. Look,
I cut myself shaving, I will say. Yes,
I have a pimple on my nose. It is a
meager attempt to take control of
a situation out of your control. You
provide a narrative. I meant for this
mistake to happen. Look, I said at
the reading, see anything different?
The students gathered around the
table stared at me, at my face. I then
launched a smile that morphed
instantly into a leer, the droopy side
of my face drooping as the muscled
side flex. My students effortlessly
generated recognizable expressions
of surprise, concern, puzzlement,

even shock. I told them it was
Bell's palsy. I have Bell's palsy. And
rehearsed for them the sudden onset,
the diagnosis, its duration. A few
then related stories of their own or
family member's palsies in the past,
attempting to re-create the uncanny
sensation of sensing through
absence, being made conscious of
the unconscious world that usually
envelopes us. A meta-discussion
for a meta-face. We thought, my
students said, you looked different.
You looked, they said, more tired.
During the readings, I did slump in
my chair. A week into the event I was
weakened by being weakened this
way. A reading is not quite theater,
a stepchild of a platform. I listened
to poetry and prose, reacting to the
words with delight and sadness. I was
conscious of the masks masking my
face, my faces.

>

I posted my face on Facebook. I
was fishing for comments. I took the
picture staring into the iMac's screen
camera in my office at home. The
afflicted half of my face is catching
light from the window that flattens
it. That side is flattened further
by the contrast with the rumpled
topography of the other side, all
valleys and peaks. Comments
began to be posted. They were
mini-memoirs mostly, mapping the
commentator's own bout with the

palsy. It was how we take these little things for granted until . . . the curl of a lip. The unconscious blink. The eyebrow arch of surprise. The scowl. The lost repertoire of our character, characters. Coming face to face with this stranger under the skin.

More or Less

The Camouflage Schemes of the Fictive Essay

The essay feigns linear narrative but initiates if not a circular notion of narrative time at least an oxbowed doubling back and forth. The essay purports to document Vonnegut's journey to Pennsylvania, there to remember with his old war buddy, Bernard V. O'Hare, the details of the bombing of Dresden in order for the author to write the book. Within the journey from Cape Cod to Pennsylvania, two meanders are recounted. Vonnegut is accompanied by two little girls, his daughter and her friend, who, he tells us, have never ventured from Cape Cod in their brief lives and who had "never seen water in that long and narrow, unsalted form before." There was a lot to see, he says. And he "sees," himself, once again through the new lenses of the children. One does not step into the same river twice. It is time to go, he tells the girls. It is always time to go. And, later, after the visit, on the return trip, crossing the Delaware at Washington's Crossing, the pilgrims visit the World's Fair, the other eddy in the stream, and there we are told of the dramatic and corporate representations of the past and the future in the present moment that Vonnegut metaphors and maps into a Mobius river of time: "how wide it was, how deep it was, how much was mine to keep."

"'I don't know anything about it,' he said. 'That's your trade, not mine.'" Writing is depicted as a "trade" and the writer as a tradesman whose expertise is the transformation of fleeting experience into solid, stable reality. Bernard V. O'Hare, who is said to have said the words above, is a prosecutor as well who uses words and witnessing to convict in the fictive theater of a courtroom. But it is not true that this is not his trade. He too is a storyteller. He too trades in the blurred boundaries between fact and fiction. He has fooled himself, however, into believing he deals only in facts. His critique has to do with the sorting of many kinds of truth, the truth and the whole truth. Prosecutor O'Hare's brief essay foils the larger essay by suggesting that there are essays and then there are essays. There is truth and the whole truth. The essays composed for his courtroom, his trade, he suggests, are the naked truth, not tailored, stable. True truth, not the disguised truth of fiction.

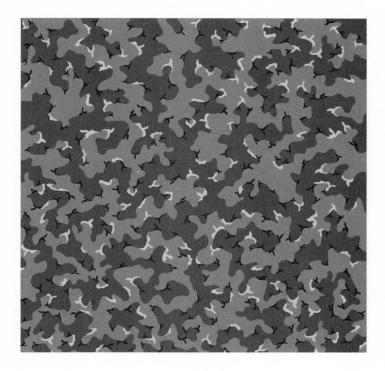

The essay disguises itself in the remnants of its own criticism and
through elaboration it recounts its own failure to recount the
failure of the writing of the fiction. The book it introduces is a
failure, Vonnegut writes at the end of the essay that recounts the
series of failed attempts to write the book that, in the end, turns
out to be a failure. The essay attempts to animate the obsessive
looping sensation of survivor guilt. Vonnegut regards his survival
of the massacre meant to kill him as a failure of the massacre.
"Everybody is supposed to be dead, to never say anything or
want anything ever again." There has been a mistake. There has
been a mistake. And the essay attempts to attempt not to rectify
the mistake but to map its own paradoxical logic, the infinite,
circling loop. He concludes by writing that the book will stand
as a failure, because it was written by a pillar of salt, another of
Vonnegut's disguises, a ruin that fragments, yes, and finally, like
the book it inhabits and the essay it embodies, melts.

"All this happened, more or less." This is the actual first line of the
book *Slaughterhouse-Five* by Kurt Vonnegut though if you ask
people they will tell you they believe that the first line of the book
Slaughterhouse-Five is this: "Listen: Billy Pilgrim has come unstuck in
time." I myself believed this. I remembered inexactly, remembering
that the section of the book, *Slaughterhouse-Five*, that begins with "All
this happened, more or less" was some kind of auxiliary writing, an
essay, an introduction to the novel that began at its conclusion: Listen:
Billy Pilgrim has come unstuck in time. But the essay that begins
the book beginning with the line "All this happened, more or less" is
a faux introduction. It pretends to introduce the novel, a nonfiction
enabling device, a frame, a context for the fiction. But, it is a
nonfiction fiction embedded in fiction. It is an introduction hidden in
plain sight. There, free-floating above the first line, "All this happened,
more or less," is not the titular banners INTRODUCTION or PROLOGUE
or PREFACE but the honest announcement of novelistic chapter: ONE.
The essay, disguised as an introductory essay, is an introductory essay
that is really a novel's chapter disguised as an essay.

"All this happened, more or less." A fact is a thing done. Finished. Something that has happened, more or less. A fiction is a thing made. Fabricated. Oddly, once something has happened, in fact, that fact no longer exists. We are left with the residue, more or less, of its happening, the physical evidence of the happening but not the happening itself as the happening has, already, happened. That residue, that evidence, can be faked, manipulated, distorted, counterfeited. The essay, nonfiction, that opens the fiction, *Slaughterhouse-Five*, constructs a spectrum right at the start. It suggests that all of this book, even the "nonfiction" part of it, is, in fact, fiction, a made thing, more or less. The book creates the pattern of ombre. The essay is a fictive essay. It is to be about blending. It is about the collaboration of corroboration. It feathers and shingles. It is about shading shading. It shades shading.

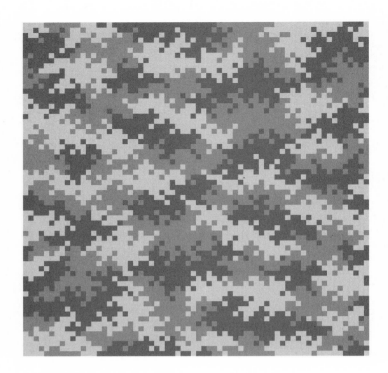

The essay suggests that it is a report of its research. It is in the
guise of a "finding." The essay titled ONE, the opening chapter
of Kurt Vonnegut's novel *Slaughterhouse-Five*, allows that it will
recount the various research methodologies the author resorted
to in order to write the book that follows. Fact-finding trips.
Note-taking and outlining. It should be read, it suggests, as a
kind of after-action report. The opening essay ends, quoting the
opening line and the last line of the novel that is to follow. This
suggests that though the essay appears at the front of the book it
was most likely written after the writing of the book it seems to
introduce. It can be read then as a kind of memory of memory.
Or memory cloaked in memory. It is the novel's memoir. But if it
is the novel's memoir it is to be read not so much as a reflection
on the past but a premonition of a future, a future that is about
the past and is about to pass. Not about the writing of the book
but about the writing about the writing of the book.

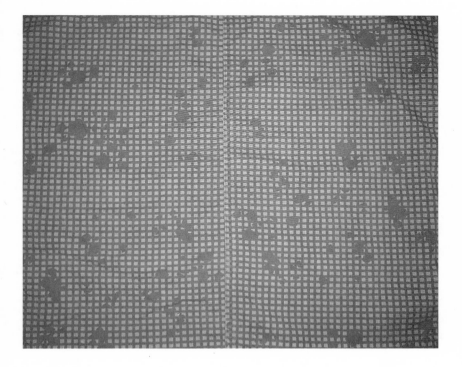

The essay that begins *Slaughterhouse-Five* assumes that it contains
a polemic aspect but then argues against itself. Kurt Vonnegut
introduces Harrison Starr, a filmmaker, the executive producer of the
polemic movie *Zabriskie Point*, who asks, "Is it an anti-war book?" to
which Vonnegut says he says that yes, he guesses it is. Starr engages
in the argument, contributes to the drama by dismissing the validity
of genre, the efficacy and aesthetic of the rhetoric of argument. He
says he says to people who say they want to write an anti-war book,
"I say, 'Why don't you write an anti-glacier book instead.'" Vonnegut
goes on to interpret, concurring with Starr's allegoric assessment that
there would always be wars and that they would be as easy to stop
as glaciers. But is this a ruse? By being amenable to the rhetorical
position of being "anti" to the "anti," one can contest it, confront the
appeal to futility. Is it about stopping the glacier or propelling it
forward? Is the book the immovable object or irresistible force? Or
both at the same time? What's that Frost said about the poem: Like
a piece of ice on a hot stove the poem must ride on its own melting.
Glacial essays as well.

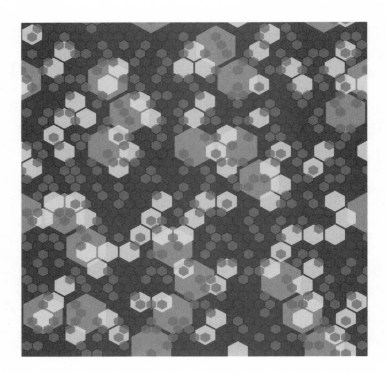

The existential nature of the artistic medium called writing is linear.
It wants to move directionally. It wishes to go someplace. There is a
beginning, middle, end. Literally, we read, in English, beginning at
the top of the page moving our eyes left to right in lines that ladder
down the page. We turn the page from right to left. The essay we read
at the beginning of the fiction *Slaughterhouse-Five* might be a hack
disguised as an essay to scramble the conventional code of the way
the novel is to be read. The essay as saboteur. The essay infiltrates and
makes possible a disruption of forward flow. It inscribes and antici-
pates skipping and stuttering. It is to get us ready for the unstuckness.
It unsticks us. A river when one looks at it, moves and does not move,
fluid and static. A glacier, too, is the embodiment of static and yet is
in a constant motion. Language wants to line up, to lead someplace, to
begin and conclude. Narrative by its nature. The lyrical essay attacks
the line, in the wolf's clothing of narrative, creates the illusion of the
line that is actually a broad and rising tide. Blot instead of plot. It
appears to condense and compress. No way out of its specific gravity,
only in deeper, a black hole, going nowhere fast.

Vonnegut's essay is an accident. My essay about that essay is an accident. Accident as an accident. Things happen in his essay and in my essay, more or less. "Accident" stumbles into the essay as a charming mistranslation by a Dresden cabdriver in his Christmas card note to Vonnegut: *If the accident will*. Vonnegut picks this up immediately and begins to worry it, adding the phrase and the pattern of accident to the weave of the writing. Writing is the willing of accident. Accident the engine of will. Will the signpost of the future. Will the document of the dead. Living will. Improvisation, accident, here is being cultured as not simply the technique but the aesthetic goal. "It is so short and jumbled and jangled . . ." Vonnegut writes about the book and about the essay that introduces the book. It is the costume of the controlled crash.

The illusion of forward momentum that masks the desired circular nature, the essay that opens the book *Slaughterhouse-Five*, contains many rounds, many endings that are also beginnings. It repeats and refrains. The essay might be thought of as a staging platform, a work bench, scaffolding, and an assembly line to construct the one perfect phrase that encapsulates the lyrical essence, vibrates the emotional resonance, and becomes Vonnegut's signature chord. "So it goes," that phrase, the incantatory Kyrie of the book and, escaping from the book into the vernacular, is formulated in the opening essay. It seems to be a mutation of an utterance that appears earlier in the essay and is repeated, "and so on." Repeating encourages experimentation with inflection and, oddly, at the same time, the flattening of inflection. Repetition flattens, bleeds the meaning out of the abstract scratches on the page. Empties it of meaning. Perhaps the only function of the essay was to be this ugly oyster with an irritant that spits out this pearl. Persistent. A perfect cyst.

The painter Abbott Handerson Thayer, considered the father of
camouflage, is the first to theorize disguise, his major book being
Concealing-Coloration in the Animal Kingdom (1909). While interested
in disruptive camouflage or dazzleflage and mimicry, his main
contribution was in the art of countershading. As a painter, Thayer
employed the technique of chiaroscuro, creating the illusion of
volume and depth on two-dimensional surfaces. Countershading in
nature, the brown back and white belly of a deer, reverses the illusion,
flattening the three-dimensional animal. Such tinkering confuses
foreground and background and depth of field. Sunlight falling on
a deer's brown back whitens, matching the white of its belly below,
flattening the silhouette, making it much more difficult to take its
range. The splotchy spots of military camouflage countershade, light
the dark valleys and blacken the lit peaks of the uniform's draping.
The soldier flattens and blends, the foreground sifting into the
background. Here, in what ways are the truths flattened or highlighted,
countershaded with the fictions? Camouflage is designed to conceal,
but can the understanding of the mechanism of perception that
explains its use be reversed? Can it be engineered to reveal?

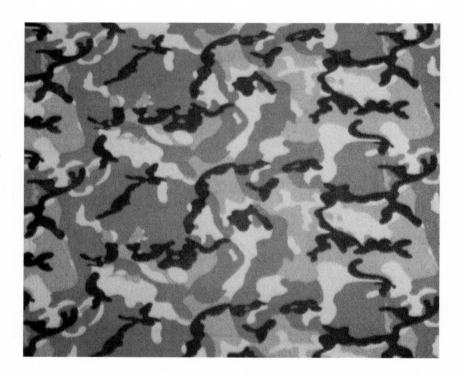

The essay is its own origin story. It also explains the origin of *Slaughterhouse-Five*'s alternate title, *The Children's Crusade*, and connecting that explanation to the origin of the book's dual dedication, for Mary O'Hare, Bernard V. O'Hare's wife, and Gerhard Müller, the Dresden taxi driver whose first appearance in the book, on the dedication page four pages before the beginning of the essay, advertises their reality before they are introduced as characters in the narrative of the trailing essay. We have no reason to believe that Vonnegut made these two characters up, but he does deploy them as characters within the essay. He is as he says in the essay: "a trafficker in climaxes and thrills and characterization and wonderful dialogue and suspense and confrontation . . ." The nonfiction of the essay enables the fiction in the way the nonfiction of the event, the firebombing of Dresden, its irreal reality, enables the fiction.

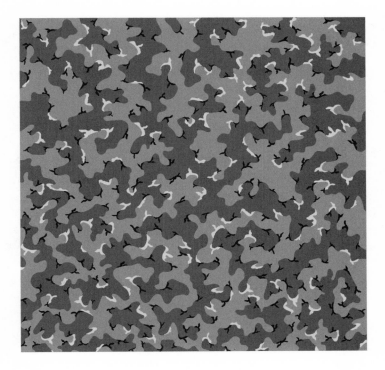

The writer Kurt Vonnegut writes that he has written this book, *Slaughterhouse-Five*, within which this essay about the writer and what he has written appears. The opening essay identifies the real drama of the book, which is not the firebombing of Dresden or The War or War so much as it is the agony, the struggle, of writing. The character "Kurt Vonnegut" that Kurt Vonnegut has written, appears in different writerly guises. He writes that he has written public relations. He writes that he wrote as a newspaper reporter for Chicago's City News Bureau. He writes that he writes letters. He writes that he wrote as a creative writing teacher at the famous Writers' Workshop in Iowa. And, of course, he is the writer of this book, *Slaughterhouse-Five*, you are reading, that seems to be being written as you are reading it. Having created the character of the writer, the writer launches the written writer into the body of the book, where he makes cameo appearances ("That was I. That was me. That was the author of this book"). As a character he traffics with Kilgore Trout, a writer of science fiction, whose day job is the delivery of news as well as the double-agent propagandist, the Air Force historian attempting to write his book about Dresden, and novelists from the planet Tralfamadore.

A pilgrimage is about being unstuck but also being stuck. It is travel and velocity but also about stasis and staying still, the station stops. The movement of the pilgrim is not sustained but constantly interrupted, by design. Vonnegut's essay is a travel essay essay. The trip from Cape Cod to Pennsylvania with many stops and starts. The trip to Dresden. The telephonic transportation of the late-night calls. The letting in and out of the dog. As we read we move through the text but we are delayed by its bafflement. We are baffled. At the beginning of the essay, Vonnegut and O'Hare have reached Dresden and tour the modern city with the cab driver Müller. And there is the side trip considering the Crusades, the spatial and spiritual pilgrimage infused with belligerent invasion. Specifically, the Children's Crusade, which was a perversion of the perverse pilgrimages that were the Crusades. The essay ends with Vonnegut making the trip to the trip to Dresden and getting waylaid in transit, stuck in a Boston motel, a non-person. There he reads three books about being marooned in time and space and genre, stalled, in between the in-between. Where is this essay located? It is perhaps a non-essay essay. Not a fiction but also not not a fiction.

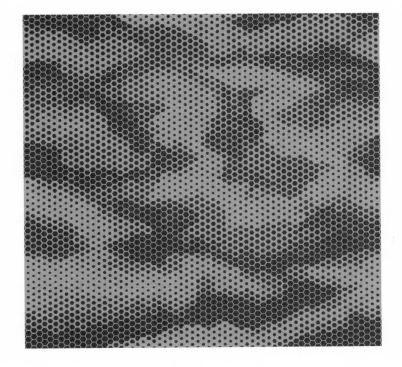

From *Slaughterhouse-Five*, the novel written in the
form described within it:

Billy Pilgrim can't read Tralfamadorian, of course, but he could, at least,
see how the books were laid out—in brief clumps of symbols separated
by stars. Billy commentated that they might be telegrams. There are no
telegrams on Tralfamadore. But each clump of symbols is a brief urgent
message—describing a situation, a scene. We Tralfamadorians read them
all at once not one after the other. There isn't any particular relationship
between all the messages, except that the author has chosen them carefully
so that when seen all at once they produce an image of life that is beautiful
and surprising and deep. There is no beginning no middle no end no
suspense no moral no causes no effect. What we love in our books
are the depths of many marvelous moments seen all at one time.

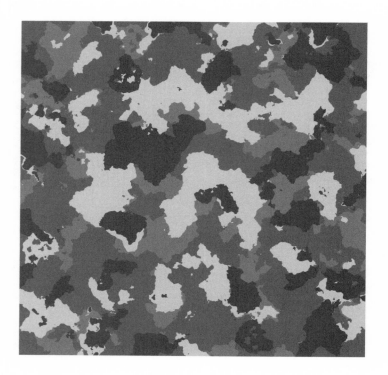

This could be a fairytale for all the gift exchange going on and
the essay nothing more than an elaborate thank-you note or a
dramatization of the thank-you note. The propellant of the action
of the essay, the trip to Dresden and the subsequent breaking of
Vonnegut's writer's block, was the Guggenheim gift money. God love
it, he writes. Later he writes: "Somewhere in there a nice man named
Seymour Lawrence gave me a three-book contract . . ." Then there
is the strange exchange (can we call it a gift exchange?) of prisoners
on the Elbe, outside Halle. Vonnegut arrives at Bernard V. O'Hare's
house "carrying a bottle of Irish Whiskey like a dinner bell." There is
this too, the part where they "give up" on remembering. Lewis Hyde
in his book *The Gift* calls gifts "erotic property," meaning that gifts are
property that stay in motion. The gift itself, the thing, is worthless.
It is only in the exchange and in motion that it is valuable. The
exchange binds us together. The essay moves and moves.
It is relentless in its motion but like a planet, a galaxy spinning,
it creates a stasis, a dynamic standstill, at its core.

I like how the essay infects the fiction of the novel that follows after it.
It infiltrates the seams and the seems of the novel. The essayistic voice
returns with a vengeance to open the tenth chapter of *Slaughterhouse-
Five* with the news bulletin of Robert Kennedy's assassination,
coupled with the current events of Martin Luther King's death and
the dead in Vietnam. The "I" assigned to Vonnegut is like a needle,
hypodermic and sartorial. The "I" proceeds to memoir and his father's
death and returns once more to the return trip to Dresden with his
buddy Bernard V. O'Hare. Interlarded with the essayistic paragraphs
are the final anecdotes of Billy Pilgrim and the witnessing of the
exhumation of the corpse mines of Dresden. "The *I* instead of the
eye," the New Journalism famously asserted, reacting to the irreality
of the Vietnam War, borrowing and importing the techniques of
fiction into the realm of nonfiction. But here in the midst of the same
moment Vonnegut reverses that osmosis, a new new journalism,
that filters back into the novel the hybridized concoction of fact and
fiction but gauged now to snag time while always letting it go.

Dear Miss Hamilton,

Where are you? In 1957, ninety years old, you are berthed in the Delphi Suite of the Greek luxury liner the ss *Queen Frederika* at sea en route to Athens, where your translation of Aeschylus's *Prometheus Bound* will be performed at the Herodes Atticus beneath the Acropolis. You are expecting Blanche Yurka, the actor cast as Io, who will broach the delicate subject of abbreviating the play before the performance. I know you will say *Cut!* All the geography can go. You amaze me. That, you, the author, well, you are not the author, Aeschylus is of course the author, the translator, then, you the translator would so severely cut her words astonishes me. This description of a city, a town, this mountain range here, all of it was long ago local color, parochial interest. You would cut all of it!

Miss Yurka played a cow, a cow in such a classic theatrical production. Such stock livestock is always a result of a fallout between Zeus, who desires, it seems, anyone and everyone, and Hera, the constantly betrayed and vengeful wife. Hera was known as the "Cow-eyed One," so perhaps being a bovine was not that bad? But the speeches are only mooing travelogues of the cow's flight to Asia, the gadfly stinging her on. It reads almost like modern advertising. "Be sure to stop at this sacred grove." "This water nymph is standing by to help you." "That temple is open late." No, these bits and pieces were all expendable.

Prometheus Bound is the actors' worst nightmare, the director's dead end. There is no action! It is like this letter to you there in the Delphi Suite on the ss *Queen Frederika*. Out to sea, indeed. Nothing going on but making speeches about speeches. Where is the action to act in that? The play is merely a bundle of recitations—don't get me wrong, these speeches contain some of the most magnificent poetry ever written and its themes are universal, timeless—with little drama. Prometheus is shackled to a mountain right from the start—very hard to act when wrapped in chains—though I bet those new method actors would want to give it a go with their eyebrows alone. Miss Yurka will have a rough enough time engaging the audience with a stock-still cow decked out in horns just trying to keep her balance on buskin hooves and mooing out a pretty speech.

You must have been flattered, moved that this translation will be performed there at the Herodes Atticus, at the foot of the Acropolis, but I am surprised that this was the play chosen. Think, this play was written twenty-five hundred years ago and translated by this ninety-year-old woman from, of all places, Indiana, about as far away from Acadia as one could get.

But there, in a place called Fort Wayne, you read ancient Greek and Latin, Hebrew, and even a little Sanskrit in your father's library. Rustic? Bucolic? You bet. No schools to speak of then. It was after the war, yes, the Civil War, in the shadow of all those depressions, economic, emotional. And yes, there were cows, like Dame Io, roaming the downtown streets, the front yards. And you put on your own plays, with your sisters and brother, your own actors and audience.

Did you think about those years in Indiana so far away now in time and space? Back then and back there, what was it you felt, so far away in time and space, reading Hesiod and Horace in the garden, marching in your imagination with Xenophon's ten thousand to the sea?

And there you were, there in the Delphi suite, looking back into the past, looking forward to Athens and this grand performance you cut down to size.

You will be led to the stage. The king of Greece will give you some sort of cross. The stoa above the theater, the Parthenon, and the Temple of Zeus will be flooded with lights for the first time. And you will be made a Citizen of Athens. A Citizen of Athens, of the city you have for so long loved as much as your own country. A piece of paper from the mayor. It will be "the proudest moment of your life" or some such. Another speech. Speeches are only speech we must remember. But we also will never forget the stages, the places the speech is given. The context. The where. The where where.

I Kill My Grandma Once and for All

If a university teaches one anything it is that the maternal grandmother is the best family member to kill. Her funeral and your attending it is a near perfect alibi for missing a class, for leverage to extend a real deadline. Her last name is different from your last name. You weren't close. She lived in another state. Not that broken up by the death? It wasn't sudden, you can say. She lingered. But briefly. Didn't suffer. Was quite old. She was ready to go. We all were ready for her to go. It is good she's at rest. But she'll be missed. You are missing her now.

I have taught for thirty years at several different universities, and I have nodded soberly and sympathetically at the news of a grandmother's passing, two or three a term. The true beauty is that the actuarial demographics are such that the there is a good chance that an actual grandmother has died. By now, too, the excuse has become a self-conscious strategy, such a cliché that the excuse is proffered with quotation marks attached, like wreaths hung around the words. "My grandmother died." Everyone is in on it. I am not a cop. I let the news, true or not, lubricate an excused absence.

In those several universities where I've worked, I have taught a class called Contemporary Rural and Agricultural Literature. At Iowa State, where I developed the class, the students mostly hailed from farms, while at Harvard, Syracuse, Alabama, and Cornell College the students reflected the more normal norm. Few, if any, students in those classes were from farms. Almost all were two or more generations away from farming, which meant that in this class, unlike a creative writing class that produces its own textbooks with the student writing, I had "content" to consider. I would be able to teach them things like what silage is. What is a haymow? What is the difference between a barrow and gilt? How does one detassel the corn? These modern urban students discovered quickly that elemental matters, matters of life and death, had long been abstractions for them. They were alienated, of course, by the culture they inhabited, and the class sought to ask and answer very basic questions: What is a farm? What is food? What do we mean by "family"?

One book we read was Mary Swander's *Driving the Body Back*, a book of poems in which the poet and her aunt drive the poet's mother's body across Iowa to be buried in the family graveyard. The car trip frames a movable wake where the other poems recount the lives and deaths of other family members already buried in the plot. At Syracuse University, the fifty students, most of them from Long Island or New York City, were many years away from farming. I asked them if they understood the book's setup, the death in Iowa City and the odyssey back home.

Yes, yes, they said, we understand that but, they asked, can you do that?

Do what? I asked.

Drive a dead person around in the back of the station wagon?

Of course you can, I said. It is, after all, your body or your family's body. We have forgotten now that the usual practice is to sign the body over to someone who "undertakes" the responsibility for burial.

I alerted them to other occasions in class where they would confront such "content." In the movies we would watch in class—*The River, Heartland, Northern Lights*—there would be graphic depictions of animal birth and slaughter. I told them to consider the distances we have all traveled from these primal occasions of the world.

Only a month before, a few weeks before the start of the semester, I got the call from my mother in Indiana letting me know my grandmother, her mother, was dying and that I should make arrangements to come home quickly if I wanted to see her alive one last time.

I made it home in time. "In time" was what my mother said, what all my family said, as they described, what looked to them to be, my grandmother's struggle to stay alive long enough for me to attend. Though she was unconscious, fighting for each breath as if each breath was indeed the last one, she seemed to know, they said, and they said they told her that Michael was on his way. She labored in the bed as I got to its side, and I remember thinking how similar this labor was to the other labor I had recently witnessed, my wife giving birth to our son.

The whole family was at my grandmother's bedside now, and now all of us were urgently whispering to her to stop, to just go. Everything was good now. Michael is here. We are all here. Rest. We hushed and whispered as she gasped, struggled. Soothed and touched. Held her hands and did not let go even after she did, finally, let go.

I was thirty-one years old, and I realized, then, that though I had seen the representations of thousands of deaths this was the first real one I had ever witnessed. I said this to the farm class then as we puzzled over Swander's book. I said my grandmother died. I smiled hearing myself recite the line. The students smiled back in recognition. And I asked them if anyone had actually seen someone die, a real death, and to ask them to think about the hundreds, the thousands of staged deaths they had seen in their lives. Not one of the fifty students, when they thought about it, had seen someone die. I recounted hoarsely my recent trip home and the raw details of my grandmother's dying, ending with the image of my mother signing the papers next to her mother's deathbed and her mother's still warm body, signing the papers for the undertaker to undertake.

What Was on My Mind

Face to Facebook with My Mother's Death, July 2012

7/9 Every month my mother recorded a clever little couplet greeting on the answering machine. Here's July . . .

> Hi, this is Patty,
> Light the sparklers, unfurl the flags, breakout the red white and blue. Leave your name and number, and we'll get back to you.

We don't have her collected works, alas.

7/9 In college my mother memorized *The Littlest Angel* and recited it to various civic and church groups. They would pay her in handkerchiefs. She continued to deliver the story year after year. She leaves us with a chest of drawers filled with handkerchiefs.

> "Well, there was a butterfly with golden wings, captured one bright summer day on the high hills above Jerusalem, and a sky blue egg from a bird's nest in the olive tree that stood to shade his mother's kitchen door. Yes, and two white stones, found on a muddy river bank, where he and his friends had played like small brown beavers, and, at the bottom of the box, a limp, tooth-marked leather strap, once worn as a collar by his mongrel dog, who had died as he had lived, in absolute love and infinite devotion."

7/10 My mother taught freshman high school English. Growing up, I was allowed to "cut" my grade school class and go to school with her. We would prep her lessons, reading at the kitchen table in the Spring Street house. One book we did every year was *Our Town*. We both took all the parts and read together the whole play. I remember the line (I think it was Emily's) "Am I pretty, Mother? Am I really pretty?" I read. And you all know what my mother's line was in return.

7/10 My mother tap-danced through the Great Depression and the war. I have a picture of her in the spangled costume in my office at school. She was fifteen dancing at a USO. Soon after I started walking, my mother outfitted me with tap shoes. I was a poor student, though I took lessons for several years. I mastered shuffle ball change but that is about all. My amazed friends would sit in the basement stairwell to watch me practice in the kitchen. At the end of the routine all the cabinet doors had popped open. Mother laughed and laughed. You dancers, you know who you are, it is all about the time step. If you can get the time step you get it all.

7/11 The first "story" story I wrote when I knew I was going to be a writer was titled "Story Problems." It was published in *Mississippi Valley Review*, long gone (Thank You MVR!). It was a collage, the sections written in the form of story problems. It concerned the memories of a math teacher (not a writer like me) trying to recall his mother, who in the story had recently died. So the sections flashed to images of the mother, the general theme being that memory is a calculus, approaching but never reaching the limit. One memory was watching his mother write checks and balancing the checkbook, the way her hand moved and the way she smoked and the way her head moved as she wrote. Many of you know that I write a lot of postcards. And as I write them I think of that image, watching my mother write by hand (as I write by hand) with our whole bodies. I wrote that story in 1979, a son beginning to write even then trying to remember his mother writing writing writing.

7/11 A few days before my mother died early Monday morning, she sent her column into the *News-Sentinel*. On the big old calendar she used to keep track of all things, I found a note she had written—"Tell Leo (her editor at the *N-S*) to run before the 11th." She had something brewing for the end of this week and wanted to get some word out. I called the editor to tell him about the deadline (interesting word) request. He told me that Mom had already let him know about getting it in print by today. If you find the article and get to the end she mentions Parkview Hospital; ever attuned to the dramatic, Mother would be taken there last Sunday morning to begin her last full day on earth:

Article no longer available

7/11 You kids today, you don't remember that The March of Dimes was once The Mothers' March of Dimes and that it consisted of mothers going door-to-door collecting change to combat first polio and then, after the vaccine, aid in neo-natal and well-baby health. My mother, after she got home from teaching at Central, took me along as she made the rounds on the March. She let me ring the doorbells. Many of them were lit from within and painted with crescent moons and when you pushed the button, the soft bell sounding inside, the light would dim. And up in the sky a real gibbous moon looked like a vaccination scar on your arm. And later she would let me count all the nickels, dimes, and quarters. She asked, "What's the take?" And I'd tell her. And then she "changed" the change into paper and let me take all the coins to my room in a Toni Dairy ("Toni Dairy—Always Ahead!") milk bottle. On the dresser, the change in the glass bottle sparked in the moonlight. It seemed to me then that we had walked for miles and touched $4.44 worth of moons. And I retraced the journey, step by step. Cars springing on Spring Street. Through all the twitchy dreams and the copper-scented night until moon rise, the rosy-fingered yawn, the next morning.

7/12 For years now, I have come home in the fall to do what I call The Double-Wide World Tour of Indiana. Mother would loan me her car, a 2000 red red vw New Beetle, and I would drive around the state giving readings at colleges and libraries for a week. Mom came along on some of these gigs, my roadie. At Butler, her alma mater, one time she was gifted with Steak 'n Shake coffee mugs. Another time, outside of Huntington, we were stuck when the state road crews blew up a bioherm during the construction of the Highway of Vice Presidents. Dan Quayle hovered overhead in a Marine helicopter. Combines were combining the cornfields on what had been once the bottom of an ancient inland sea. We followed the Wabash and the canal across the state heading home, north-northeast, the glacial plain gently drifting away from us off the port beam, the sun setting, redder than the Bug, through the million flat flat strata of dusty dust.

7/12 My mother was a high school freshman English teacher. Her high school freshman English teacher was Mrs. Wiggs, who was, years later, my freshman English teacher at Franklin Junior High. In her class, I memorized Shakespeare (the prologue of *Romeo and Juliet*) and was introduced to the short story: "The Necklace," "The Interloper," "The Gift of the Magi," "The Lottery," "The Lady or the Tiger." Mrs. Wiggs always would remind me that my mother, years before, had read and recited these very lessons. I was, I am, a terrible speller. Mrs. Wiggs, at the end of her rope one day, took my hand and breathed into it—"WHERE" and "WERE"—do you feel the difference? she would say. Whhhhere and were. I thought of her today because I am wondering how to do the viewing later today, and then I remembered how Mrs. Wiggs did it when her husband, Bill, died. My mother and I went to the funeral home and Mrs. Wiggs greeted us and reminded me of my spelling shortcomings gently. "Come, let's go visit Bill." And we walked over to the casket. How strange this visitation, yes? I guess I will take up hundreds of hands today, leading you to the far end of the big room. Where. Were. There is a part of me that still, after all these years, wants to confuse the spell.

7/12 Tomorrow, the Mass. There will be three readings. The first from Job 19:1, 23–27:

> O would that my words were written down! Would that they were inscribed in a record: that with an iron chisel and with lead they were cut in rock forever! But as for me, I know that my Vindicator lives, and that he will at last stand forth upon the dust whom myself shall see: my own eyes, not another's, shall behold him and from my flesh I shall see God. My inmost being is consumed with longing.

7/13 My mother was upset that in my book *MICHAEL MARTONE* there are several stories in which a character by the name of Michael Martone's Mother dies. She dies by cancer, by cold. She wastes away. There is an accident. In one, Michael Martone is not a writer but a ditch digger who digs ditches all over the world only to return home to dig the ditch where Michael Martone's Mother would be buried. I tried to calm my mother when she read all these depictions of Michael Martone's Mother's death. I said to her many times that it was true she dies but in the next story she returns for a new adventure, a little narrative where she lives and where she lives still. Secretly, I was nursing that childish wish that if death came unexpectedly I could prevent it by imagining all the ways it would come. Who by fire? Who in the merry merry month of May? I meditated on many ways to die, but I missed stroke. How could I miss stroke? I know my childish answer amused my mother, and that she forgave me. She was, after all, a reader, and, even more important, a writer who, in fact, composed my life, the life of Michael Martone, and, who, in that mysterious way, wrote through me all the ways one might imagine to live and all the ways one might imagine, one day, to die.

7/14 Saturday night before she went to sleep, my mother set out her outfit for Sunday Mass. A bright red paisley jacket, white blouse and slacks, and her red Converse Chuck Taylor high tops with the contrasting lace crew socks. She died Sunday morning no doubt knowing that she had begun to organize her own funeral. We buried her in the clothes she was going to wear to church. Thank you all for allowing me, over the last few days, to share some of my mother's writing, report on her life and death, and reflect on the events of the last few days. Note that previous sentence. That would have been exactly the way my mother would have written it. Soon, I will be heading back to Tuscaloosa. I'd invite you all to come visit me in my cluttered office—many of you know what I mean by cluttered. There I would show you a photograph I have of my mother, smiling her crooked smile, sitting with her husband, my father, Tony, on their gravestone, ready to go. Ready to go. I love that still picture, the two of them balanced there, cracking up, a little creepy, a little crazy, a little irreverent. Really, stop by Morgan Hall, and we will look through all the crap I have accumulated in this life she gave me—the books and action figures, the files of papers, the cups and posters, the chairs and knickknacks. We'll take a look at that little picture, if you still have the patience, and I will go on and on and on and on about my mom. But for now I'll stop and thank you once again for your being here and bearing with me.

7/17 Michael Martone is back home in Tuscaloosa at 12:34 in the morning. A long flight from Indiana. A dash through the Atlanta airport. An uneventful drive from Birmingham home. Nick's asleep. He soon will be. The crickets and frogs are holding forth.

7/17 Miss Catherine is the Woman Who Walks in Tuscaloosa. Every day she walks back and forth, up and down Tuscaloosa. She lives nearby. Today she talked with me. I said, I know you, Miss Catherine. And she said, You don't know me. And I said, You live right up the street from me. And Miss Catherine said, I don't live there. I live right here where I am.

11/19 The Facebook Kaddish.
Today would have been my mother's eighty-second birthday. She died four, yes four, months ago. Though I am not Jewish, I have been saying the Kaddish since then at the loving suggestion of a very good friend who knew it would help to remember my mother's death daily, formally, and exclusively in my very busy life. No minion, of course, but perhaps my friends here on Facebook who, over this third of a year, also have suffered death. I still have not figured out this community online but I do know that with this mourning I have been in many ways very close to my virtual friends here. I don't know what that says about our times, but I am thankful for the digital tether, for the wistful connection in a historically centripetal age. "To the departed whom we now remember . . . may the Father of peace send peace to all who mourn and comfort all the bereaved among us."

What Was on My Mind

Face to Facebook with My Father's Death, March/April 2014

March 25. Shuttling off to Shuttlesworth.

March 28. Touch, go, touch, go.

March 30. Fourth Sunday of Lent.

March 31. Dear Friends, I am fortunate in my life to have been fathered by two extraordinary men. Unfortunately, both now are gravely ill here in Fort Wayne and Baltimore. I do not mean here to vaguebook but the situations are dynamic and complex, and it is impossible at this time to detail these moments. I know many of you know something is not quite right, a disturbance in the field, but I do and my family does appreciate your attentive and sympathetic presence. I am distracted, but I am sensing, and am deeply grateful for, your best wishes and your binding and abiding affection. I am fortunate in that regard as well.

April 3. Dear Friends, I am in another country, the country of Indiana. At times like this and in places like this, many of us turn to stories poetry language to pass the time and to pass into time. That's just the way we roll, yes, writers and readers. Last night I needed a bedtime story and the internet provided me with this one. Mr. Stacey Ketch read me to sleep. Thought I would share. Another one of these concoctions of language that helps a bit but explains nothing. Explains nothing. It's the way we roll, this muttering. I cannot resign myself.

April 4. Two pictures of my father back in the day. He was known as Junior back then. I like the little scrape on the knee. And he wore a hat well.

April 4. One memorable moment today with my father. He opened one eye, his good eye, and looked at me a moment and focused. "Nice shirt," he said. A flannel, Black Watch tartan.

April 5. My son, Sam Martone, I had hoped to be there at Arizona State to see him "defend" his fiction thesis, but I won't be able to. Too many story-lines in motion right now. I am certainly very happy that at Arizona State they seem to have thesis defense postcards. He has mailed me one. I hope he has mailed one to you. I never told him bedtime stories. We always, at bedtime, told stories together. Also he was of the first generation that used the baby crib monitor. So each night after he was put down, I could listen in to his crib narratives, wonderful monologues, detailing the day that was at night deconstructing itself. Huzzah! And remember my one piece of advice about writing: Never do anything half-assed.

April 5. Dad and I were making the rounds tonight of the third floor of the St. Anne Home, and *The Bells of St. Mary's* was showing at the movies in the lounge. *South Pacific* is the big favorite, but there was a lot of attention being paid to Ingrid and Bing. The hills were alive with the sound of saints.

April 6. Fourth night with Dad.

April 7. Last night, remembering with the amazing Ron Ryan while Dad slept, I recalled Fort Wayne's millennium celebration and how my mother insisted the events have a mascot. Her idea of a millipede named Millie carried the day, and an elaborate costume was constructed—insect-green foam rubber suit, antenna-equipped head with multiple arms connected in such a way as to simulate simultaneous movement. Dad appeared at all the events—parades, fireworks—as this creature, allowing the children to pet him or flee from him. I remember it was so hot that he would take the head off and the effect was that of being consumed bodily by a giant grub. His eyes closed, Dad, listening, still gave a little smile at that. I said, "Dad, you remember when Mom had you disguised as a giant bug don't you?" She would always imagine such missions for him. Mom loved alliteration. I asked her why it couldn't have been Milton the Millipede but, no, she thought Millie sounded better. Dad was game.

April 7. When the wind is right, I can hear even here in my father's room the fast freights of the N&S on the old Nickel Plate main running on the southern bank of the Maumee. That old urgency crossing grade level at Anthony next to the old Wayne Candy Company plant, pushing the sound of the horn ahead of it, draining onto the viaduct downtown. That takes me back to all those nights, all those trains burbling through the night through this sad and lost city.

April 7. Just now, Father Jack, the pastor of St. Anne, performed once more the anointing of the sick in his pajamas, sweat pants and an Under Armor T-shirt, a lovely dream of dream-like gestures of gestures in a room lit by computer screens and task lights and sighing sounds of the breathing of the bellows bed, the shallow panting of Father.

April 8. Just now, Paul, one of Dad's golf buddies stopped by reporting to him that Lakeside, their favorite course, is underwater. There's been hard rains yesterday and last week, and all the snow of the hard winter, the last of the piles still in the shadows, are contributing to what is, for Fort Wayne, its annual rite of spring. Flooding. You probably know this. Fort Wayne is on a continental divide, not like the one out west, all mountains, but a little lip of high ground, a matter of a couple dozen feet that separates the Atlantic from the Mississippi basin. Every spring the water rises and has to decide which way it's going to go. All the parks on the floodplain fill up with broad, shallow sheets of dazed and lazy water. Floods in Fort Wayne are always leisurely disasters, a few inches either way, a steady seeping. Steeping.

April 8. Just now, I went down to the nurse's station next to the dining room and lounge of St. Anne, second floor. I am wearing my black corduroy jacket, black pants, blue shirt, and a bow tie. I was asking after the Ativan. The dining room and lounge was packed. Lunch and midday meds and a Frank Sinatra concert tape on the big-screen TV. A physical therapist was tossing a beach ball with one of the residents. Another one looked at me and said I looked like a priest or a lawyer. Frank was singing, "I get no kick from champagne."

April 9. Unmoored, adrift, at sea.

April 9. My father, Tony Martone, died yesterday evening, 10:45 p.m., at St. Anne Home in Fort Wayne, Indiana. I thank all of my friends who sat up with us during this passage. The sky is clear. The moon is halved. All but the brightest planets and stars are washed out by the nightlights left on. It is just cold enough. This waiting is always an act of imagination.

April 10. I thought I didn't give Mother and Dad too much to worry about, but they were never happy with my hair. It was always too long, and then when I didn't cut it during the Bush administration every time they saw me lips were bit. "You can't see your face," my mother always said. Oh, I know certain traditions of mourning call for the suspension of grooming at this time, and I will be, as I did with Mother, saying the Kaddish (I'll get back to you, my Minion), but I had my hair cut today. First, I called Phil Rizzo, who is ninety, and who, until last week, was still cutting hair down on Broadway. My father took me there, years ago, for my very first haircut. Mr. Rizzo told me he'd sold his chair, his scissors. We had a great talk about Dad and Mother. His daughter, Barb, had been a student of hers at Central and had babysat me. In the end, I searched around town and found a shop near where Dad will be viewed on Sunday, Karl's, which is owned by Gary, who was the only barber left in what was once a five-chair establishment. He cut and cut and cut my hair. We talked about Dad and Fort Wayne and haircutting—the decline of barbershops and the acceleration of time in general. He also collected safes, and the empty spaces in shop were filled with huge blocks of steel vaults. It was great. I told him about the sign Mr. Rizzo had had in his shop—"Many a man thinks he's being cultivated when he is only being trimmed."

April 11. A footnote (or more exactly, a headnote) to the haircut post from yesterday. At the end of the haircut, Gary dramatically turned me around in the chair so I could see in the big mirror and stood behind me with the hand mirror so we could both admire his work. Hair everywhere on the floor, the apron. He had worked a long time with scissors, mostly, and comb. It looked good. Short but it still had some lift to it, some oomph in a wiseguy kind of do. Gary, who told me he'd been cutting hair for forty-nine years, also told me the story of how he had worked for Karl for four years before Karl retired, and Gary bought the chairs and asked Karl if he, Gary, could keep Karl's name. We admired my burnished head in the mirrors. Sharp. When I got back in the car and looked at the rearview, I noticed for the first time that the sideburns were way uneven, the right one a good inch longer than the left. I laughed and thought of James and narrative and the flaw in the carpet. I went home and used my nephew's Norelco trimmer to even them up the best I could.

April 11. My father, Tony Martone, died late Tuesday night. It took a while for the funeral home to arrive and fetch the body. I sat on the floor in the hallway outside the room where the Tuesday before he had fallen on the way to the shower. He was still trying to use the walker then, and he fell backward, away from it, into my arms, and then I fell with him, down to the floor where a week later I am waiting for the funeral home to come collect the body in the bed in room 216. And they did eventually. By then it was the next day. After they left, we collected the few things we had moved into the room to leave, leaving it even emptier. I cleared the things from the medicine cabinet in the bathroom. He had his shaver there. He had been shaved a day before he died, and I had slapped on a drop or two of the Old Spice, an almost empty bottle to be collected there, too. He always liked Old Spice. And I always liked the ivory tusk-shaped bottle with its little stopper. The faked scrimshawed clipper ship up on step sailing away. I popped the head off the razor before putting the odds and ends into the Dopp kit. Beneath the shaving heads the gray dust clump of his whiskers. My grandfather, Dad's dad, Tony, I always called Grandpa Moosh. He was blind and seldom shaved, and when I was little he would take my hands and rub them over his throat and cheeks—"Moosha, moosha," he'd say. Earlier that night I had rubbed my father's face, "moosha, moosha," I said, stirring the scent of the Old Spice, the broken accent of Grandpa Moosh. The cloud of whiskers slipped from the razor, spilled into the white white porcelain of the sink, an ashy nautical chart, an old newspaper photograph, pencil lead, steel filings, storm clouds. Out in the empty room, the room was being emptied. I turned the water on and watched the residue of all those daily rituals drain away.

April 12. Now, Mother was a writer. She wrote all the time. My earliest memories were her writing at the kitchen table in a pool of light generated by those old pull-down kitchen lamps. My father, on the other hand, barely wrote. He didn't read much either. Instead he was always moving, the athlete. The lines he made were in the grass with the mower. He was, for most of his working life, a switchman for the phone company. His connection to language was to connect other people's conversations through the old analog automatic switches in anonymous buildings all over Fort Wayne. He tended the mechanism of dialing, built little pipelines for your words to flow. But, in short, he was no reader or writer. Mother took care of that. Save twice a year, when I was in college, first at Butler and then at Indiana. My father paid my way through school by means of U.S. Savings Bonds, in twenty-five-dollar increments he had deducted from his pay. He stored the bonds themselves in a safe deposit box at the Lincoln Bank branch at Sherman and State. Each semester, I would go with him and sit across the table while he, in his painfully cramped tortured hand, affixed his signature on bond after bond. His writing was so . . . physical, Shakespearean almost, as he wrote so little his signature varied, seemed to be invented new each time he attempted it. Though the switches he tended were automatic, his signature was like the old PBX board, each call a different configuration of wires and sockets. All my books are here in the house. Signed to Mother and Dad. I doubt if he ever read them. Mother maybe read parts of them to him no doubt while he was doing something, doing something else. Moving, always moving.

April 13. In the days leading up to his death, Dad, who died on April 8 in the late evening, was often angry with me. The hospice nurse called this, sagely, "terminal agitation." I thought that was a bit clinical and removed. I was pissed, too. My father was a very polite man who occasionally had a temper, and in the final days to the nurses and aides it was still pretty much please and thank you. I took the wrath as a kind of intimacy we shared. Love expressed with this terminal anger. I don't mean to say it was huge. He mostly wanted to go home. "Mick (he called me Mick or Mickey—most folks thought this was after Mickey Mantle but it really was after a boyhood friend of his who died young, Dad serving the first time as a pallbearer), I want to go home." He was very frail and weak, but he would throw off his covers and throw his legs over the side of the bed, "Dammit, Mick, let's go!" and shoot me the eyebrows—my brother, Tim, knows this look. Now, the hospice nurse knows this move as well, saying that the dying often speak in metaphor. Home isn't home but "Home," you know. Whatever. But I did wrestle him out of bed and into the borrowed wheelchair and for the next hour or so walked around and around the second floor of St. Anne, pushing my father, going. As it turns out, one of my favorite movies is *The Wild Bunch* and the critical line in that movie is "Let's go." He fell asleep in the chair, me behind him talking as always over his PAL baseball-capped head. As I mentioned before, Dad was a fine athlete, constantly moving, going, a physical presence, and now he was calling upon the body to move again and it was not responding. It would make any of us mad. Agitated, hell yes. Today is the viewing. Right now, I am willing myself to get up out of this damned chair and begin to get ready to go. For four hours I will stand beside my Dad, stiller than still. You all know that stillness, that in-animation. Oh, we can call it sleep, metaphor it to hell, but it is stiller than still. "Mick, let's go. C'mon, Mick, please, Mick, please. Let's go."

April 14. To the hospital where dad was recovering from the infection and still in his delirium our cousin Anita brought a gift of a word puzzle book.

What are those puzzles called? The ones that are fields of seemingly random letters that have been hidden in the jumble of words that are spelled out horizontally, vertically, diagonally. What are they called? Needless to say, the codes went unbroken there. We still believed that Dad could come back, rehab, and live once again in the apartment. I transferred the book to St. Anne and it was there on the shelf next to the bed where he died, its secrets still safe. I don't know where it is now in the jumble of stuff brought home from that room. Yesterday was the visitation. Today is the funeral mass and burial. The visitation is a kind of a puzzle too. One has to, for a minute or two, puzzle, piecing together a narrative of history, connection, affection, loss, labor, disease, passion, agony, et cetera with the tools of chitchat, cliché, prayer, sighs. It is called a viewing but it is more a sounding. I barely looked at the body of my father, that wall of profound silence at my back as I whispered these combinations of letters to these complex constructions of the still-inarticulate burblings of human language. I was profoundly moved viewing the faces of those who visited, the pages of brief moments where the gestures and expression of the living revealed themselves in such raw elemental ways. I circle that one. I circle that one. That one there makes a kind of sense now. Circle that. There, there in a cloud of letters, a camouflage of script, there I see you.

April 15. It snowed overnight. Snowed! For those of you following along at home, here were the readings at Dad's funeral yesterday, 4-14-14: Lamentations 3:17–26, II Corinthians 4:14–5:1, John 11:32–45 (Jesus wept). The responsorial Psalm was number 63, I thirst. We selected that to remind us of the few days before, asking Dad if he would like some water, having him nod yes, and then when I tried to place the syringe in his mouth have him shake it off like a pitcher to a catcher. Monsignor, it turns out, had been an English major. Greeting people at the back of the church before mass, Sam and I talked with him about Sam's recent defense of his thesis, a book of stories. And Monsignor believed that Iowa was the place for creative writing instruction. We begged to differ. He was of course a fan of Flannery O'Connor. I asked him if he had ever read J. F. Powers. Anyway, he relished the passage from John as the text for the homily, and I was pleased he focused on untying Lazarus, letting him go. I mentioned earlier here that my father's last words to me were "Let's go." I told that to Monsignor earlier as we stood in the doorway at the back of the church and watched as the lid of the casket was screwed into place. So, it all worked out. A year or so ago, he worked harder in addressing Mary keeping all this in her heart at Mother's funeral, a curveball, but yesterday he was ready, as John 11, the story of Lazarus, had been the gospel at that last Sunday's Mass. It was the last Sunday my father had been alive, Palm Sunday's Palm Sunday. Dad's nephew, Joel, is a deputy sheriff, and with Dad's fifty years of connection with the Police Athletic League, the streets of Fort Wayne were cleared for the slow ride out to the cemetery, the new Dodge muscle cars leapfrogging intersection to intersection in front of the hearse. Sirens and lights. We left the casket there, a Batesville one, the Indiana company that manufactures both caskets and hospital beds, another thing I talked about with Monsignor as the casket was sealed before the pall was placed on top. Anyway, not a graveside service but there in the mausoleum. A good thing as the day had turned cold and the clouds lowered themselves getting ready for the snow— snow on April 14. I am heading south today, death and taxes. Finally, back to Tuscaloosa, home of an apparently unranked creative writing program as far as the Jesuits are concerned. In my office is one of my favorite pictures of Mother and Dad, the one where they are sitting on their gravestone, the same one they are both now lying beneath. They are laughing, laughing. They are so alive at that moment there. It is sun and no snow. The invitation still stands. Visit me in Morgan Hall and I will introduce you to that image of Mother and Dad test-driving the new ride.

April 16. Made it home to Alabama. An eleven-hour drive. I just had to say that we hit Huntsville just as the big fat moon decided to haul itself out of the Tennessee River, a mess of buttery light. And in Tuscaloosa, even in the dark, I could tell the garden decided to go on without me. And someone left a gift of a shopping cart parked near the concrete deer in the front yard. Home. Home. Home. Home.

Against the Beloved

"The man has been a joke for years!" this was the assessment given by an editor, the editor of my first book, a book of stories, as he looked through the wish list of names I had provided for him to contact as possible blurbers. The writer my editor declared had been a joke for years had been at the top of my list. The writer was Kurt Vonnegut, and the editor dismissed him, declaring him a joke, indicating he, the editor, would not even send a galley to Mr. Vonnegut, the galley wasted. This was 1983. This took place in a high-rise office in New York. What did I know? It was my first book, and this was all new to me. Looking back, I don't know why I was shocked, the editor was being an editor, exerting his taste, and this editor, perhaps more than most, was famous for such exertions, such pronouncements. I was shocked back then, however, because for all the years Mr. Vonnegut had been a joke in this office in New York (I assumed) he also had been or his writing had been so central to my writing in and about Indiana.

For years, I thought a lot about that dramatic utterance as I continued to write, and I continued to read the writing Mr. Vonnegut continued to write. And I thought about it again upon Mr. Vonnegut's death as the spontaneous assessments of mortal editors get edited to the final immortal edit. Think of today's epitaphs here as another litany of blurbs. Epitaphs, blurbs writ in stone. I see now, of course, that the editor back then was employing my naïve selection of Kurt Vonnegut and his subsequent dismissal of him as a normative occasion, a teachable moment for me as a beginning writer. He was editing, not my stories, but the budding narrative of a budding writer's life story. I was not, at the beginning of my life as a writer, to emulate such a writer who was in his opinion a joke.

But I am here to say to that editor today, thanks for nothing, pal. I am here today to say that I now understand differently what you said back then meant. I am here today to say that, yes, indeed Kurt Vonnegut had been, was indeed, and should continue to be a joke.

By that I don't mean to invoke the dismissive connotation of slight, trivial, minor (what I think the editor thought he meant by "joke"), but I do wish to invoke the profound power, the mystery of the joke and the fool who jokes, equipped with little more than jokes to address and redress the world.

I think now that the editor knew this too, labeling Mr. Vonnegut a fool when in fact the Fool, a job description for the writer the editor, a writer himself, could only aspire to. To be called a "joke" was to be identified as something other, to be banished, to be outside polite company, to be impolite, impolitic, disrespectful. To call Mr. Vonnegut a "joke" here is to assert that that role is utterly necessary and exactly what I have aspired to become as a writer.

I am quite conscious of this moment's occasion and know, I am not naïve still, that the words I speak here are to memorialize the departed and to impart a kind of lubricant to the telling transition to a lasting memory. I am to finish, finish the final finish, an ultimate application of gloss to the gloss of a life of an important man and his work. But I find I am resisting that here, resisting the application of the stain of "beloved," resisting assisting in the transformation from grub to butterfly. Let me then apologize instead of eulogize, make an argument for Mr. Vonnegut's writing as also resisting being loved, turning Mr. Vonnegut himself into the beloved Kurt Vonnegut, retaining for the moment Kurt Vonnegut's place in literary history as a deadly serious joke.

I am arguing that we are not to love, to admire, to be fond of what we find in his life and work. It is ugly, uneven, distasteful, caustic, brittle, prickly. It is raw, scored and dangerous as the potential kinetic shrapnellic energy of an unpinned fusing, fussing, and sputtering unexploded hand grenade. I want him to continue to be armed and dangerous. And such a hand grenade should not be spiked and displayed as a curious souvenir, a harmless hunk of lead, a paperweight. The man has been a joke for years and I want him to stay that way, unbeloved, grumpy, at a distance, removed, and yes, listen, unstuck.

Mr. Vonnegut went a long way in his personae to cultivate the habit of the unbeloved calling himself tirelessly an old fart steeped in Pall Malls, with breath like mustard gas and roses. His heroes define antiheroes, Billy Pilgrim, Eliot Rosewater, the double-double Nazi agent Howard W. Campbell Jr., are all "difficult" to say the least, and his alter ego, the writer Kilgore Trout, friendless and despised, a bitter man, cowardly and dangerous and obviously very good at his job, "keeps body and soul together as a circulation man for the *Illium Gazette*, manages newspaper delivery boys, bullies and flatters and cheats little kids." Trout doesn't know how many books he has written but in one written in 1932 called *Gutless Wonder* about a robot with bad breath he imagines the use of flaming jellied petroleum to burn and kill human beings. Mr. Vonnegut, though, was not a Cassandra, not doomed to not be listened to because of disturbing though accurate predictions of the future. No, I think Vonnegut was the anti-Cassandra—not believed, ignored for his disturbing though accurate panoramas of our pasts.

Pasts, usually, because they are past and glossed over, explained, digested, rendered inert as the dead decay into the beloved, dirt decomposes into nostalgic "soil," morphs into "hallowed ground." Mr. Vonnegut was and is the anti-historian, a dirty job but someone has to do it, not defusing the past but remining it in the reminding of it, resisting the sanding nature of History (with a capital H) biases to blah, to make palatable the past.

"I was there," Billy whispers to the astounded Historian and his fifth wife in the hospital who don't believe him, who diagnose him with the deflecting belittling malaise of echolalia (Echo, the love of Narcissus). They consider him mad, a liar when he witnesses about witnessing the destruction of Dresden, the destruction of Dresden that the Historian, above it all, has written and written off. I was there Billy Pilgrim says, survived traumatically the horrific there-ness of it, the therelessness of its aftermath (as did Mr. Vonnegut) survived it as a mistake, an anomaly, an outlier, an alien, as, ultimately, invisible, a ghost, as Mr. Vonnegut writes of a massacre: everybody is supposed to be dead to never say anything or want anything ever again. Everything is supposed to be very quiet after a massacre and it always is except for the birds. And what do the birds say:

I live in Alabama now and every morning I am greeted by mocking of the mockingbird that lives in the juniper bush outside my window. This mockingbird mimics the rattle and hiss of the neighborhood's air conditioners, the throaty thrum of the compressor coming on. Ms. Harper Lee often visits Tuscaloosa. Miss Nell, we call her affectionately, administers an annual essay contest on the theme of civil rights, attending the award ceremonies with breath like mustard gas and roses. She is and her book is beloved, the ugliness it depicted and dramatized, now defanged and declawed by the emery board of distance, of time. What's not to love? Who can actually route for Bob Ewell? Miss Maudie Atkinson, neighbor lady, comforts Jem after the trial, saying that his beloved father, Atticus, takes on the awful jobs that the rest of Macomb cannot face. It is Atticus that Sheriff Tate asks to shoot the rabid dog, after all. And after all that, the dog dead in the dust, Sheriff Tate tells Atticus he can let the dead dogs lie. He will send Zeebo to collect and dispose of the carcass. There are awful jobs and then are awful jobs. We can admire Atticus's aim and skill and his modesty about his proficiency.

Zeebo's task cannot be made noble but is always necessary. It is necessary and necessarily unsung, finally always, unbeloved.

Mr. Vonnegut performed Zeebo's tasks serving as a miner on the post-apocalyptic moonscape where he opened up, one after another, the corpse mines of firebombed Dresden. This irreal reality is both real and a metaphor. One could say that Mr. Vonnegut's many books are also excavations. I would also say Mr. Vonnegut models the profession of the writer as a tender of the dead, the murdered, the massacred, and the past they inhabit. He restores. He reconciles. He forgives but does not forget. The writer as mortician.

Or perhaps, more accurately, Mr. Vonnegut was an anthropologist for both the necropolis and the metropolis. Mr. Vonnegut wrote often about his training in a field whose discipline demands an unstuckness, a disinterest, a distance, and a downright dumbing down of one's own sense of being a human being by design. Anthropologists are always walking in, walking in alone, taking up residence among groups of humans with benign and genuine curiosity, with affection and attention, perhaps, but never true connection. You are the guest, the stranger, the resident alien, the scientist, the documentarian. After the corpse mines of Dresden, Mr. Vonnegut blew his GI Bill money to get a degree for something the war had already taught him in spades. The University of Chicago would grant him the formality of this formality, certifying the credentials of the walking dead, theses delivered to the social science composed of shadows, the dissertations by detached, insomniac recording angels.

I always wanted you to admire my fasting, says the dying hunger artist. Mr. Vonnegut held fast to this displaced point of view, maintained at what expense of energy, that unstuckness, that out-of-place placelessness, and was able to negotiate this nether with a kind of inhuman humanity, an inalienable alienation. I can admire him but at a distance, a distance he inscribed for himself and insisted upon others.

Mr. Vonnegut was a joke. He constructed many elaborately simple and hideously beautiful books that are jokes. We must not embrace the jokes or be buddies with them, pet them or grow comfortable with them. Or love them. They are by their nature and design off-putting.

We must continue to laugh, however, not out of respect or politeness or even love, especially not out of love, but because it was, Mr. Vonnegut has written, the first thing he heard emerging from the tomb of Slaughterhouse-Five after the end he survived. He heard laughter. He laughed. He was laughter. The laugh. The guffaw of mocking, the tickled-pink ululation, our feathered breath, our articulate inarticulation. Our Poo-tee-weet?

Finger Exercises

Tuscaloosa, April 27, 2011

It was one of the 362 tornadoes in the 2011 Super Outbreak, the
largest tornado outbreak in United States history. The tornado
reached a maximum path width of 1.5 miles during its track
through Tuscaloosa, and once again north of Birmingham, and
attained estimated winds of 190 mph shortly after passing
through the city.—Wikipedia

From the South

Not the hand of God so much as one index finger pointing, touching there
and, then, there no longer there. I always believed the digitized clouds stag-
gered, wove, wave after wave of wind. The cloud circled as it circled. But this,
this was a fist. From space, the infrared scored true, a bearing undeflected,
the deep crease in the palm, read, ruled.

Southwest

Disaster skins paper. Unbinds it. Its wake is a wake of paper. Waste balled up.
Drifting into drifts, sheets shifting in the leftover wind. Left like leaves in the
stripped-bare branches of trees. Files. Receipts. Photographs. Prescriptions.
Directions. Notes. Greeting cards. Menus. Letters. Lists. Lists. Pages sloughed
from books and Bibles found miles away, smoothed by a hand, dog-eared,
thumbed through, blotted, hung out to dry, amateur restoration in order to
turn in, to turn back, to return.

To the North

On Fifteenth Street, there was a neon sign, a pharmacy's mortar and pestle,
flashing. The light strobing created the illusion of someone's invisible hand
stirring. The storm settled here on this spot. And ground. Ground. Ground.
Ground. Ground.

Northeast

My finger on the remote button pressed rewind over and over and rewound the wind. The wound undone. Took the wind out of the wind. Outside, the mockingbird stuttered on the sagging cable.

Postcards from Below the Bug Line

The Site of Contestation

For a while there, I taught in the English Department of Syracuse University, but back then it wasn't really an English Department. It was the Department of English and Textual Studies. We had given up studying literature with a coverage model—too much of it to go over, questions of canon formation—and instead we were teaching ways of reading that could be applied to any text, literature or not. What that meant was that, say, one semester no classes on Shakespeare would be offered, while in the next semester there would be three or four, covering the same texts but each through a different lens. There would be a Marxist interpretation or a feminist one. Race would be the focus of a third, or queer theory.

My colleagues would argue about what they called the "site of contestation," the essential element of identity, the way meaning was going to mean. Was it class, gender, race?

I weighed in or maybe waded in to the argument by offering place as a possible other site to contest. My colleagues found this highly amusing. The notion that regionalism would ever be used as a primary interpretative textual tool was ludicrous to them, even as I pointed out, only half in jest, that real political power is still connected to place. We vote in precincts and wards, in jurisdictions, in counties, in states. But our identifying with a place seems now only an adjectival afterthought at best. I am (and we can and do argue over the order of the initial descriptors) a white male middle-class straight cisgendered writer. Where and when would I add that I am also a Hoosier, a Midwesterner to boot? Or a Southerner, now that I have lived and have worked in a place—Tuscaloosa, Alabama—for as many years as I lived and worked in Indiana?

The Ruined Folly of Foster Auditorium

That year, 2008, I wore a suit and tie to vote.

My polling place, as it has been for the last ten years, was Stillman College's Hay Hall. Stillman College is a historic black college established by northern white Presbyterian abolitionists during Reconstruction on the Heights in the West End of Tuscaloosa. Eighteen years ago, I, a northern white liberal, moved into the neighborhood. The West End is literally the wrong side of the tracks. It was also the *de jure* black precinct of the town and is, today, still the *de facto* one.

The first time I showed up to vote at Stillman, I was dressed casually. I might have even had on running gear or lawn-mowing clothes in order to dart in, vote, and get back home and on with the rest of the day. I was shocked to discover that my African American neighbors—those handing out sample ballots on the way in to vote, the poll workers and observers, the other voters as well, all of them—were dressed in their Sunday-best clothes. The ladies at the table with the registration rolls even wore wide-brimmed sun hats trimmed with gardens of flowers and nests of feathers. I was shocked and embarrassed.

I hadn't expected it, obviously. And for years after, when I traveled back up north, I would dine out on that moment as my friends would ask me what it was really like living way down south. Everyone dresses up to vote, I would tell them.

It didn't take me long to figure out why. The lady highlighting my name with a ruler and a bright yellow marker that stained her cotton gloves as she crossed me off remembered when there had been no polling place on the West End, remembered one had to figure the number of nails in a keg in order to qualify to vote, remembered memorizing the entire Declaration of Independence just in case.

Outside the door of Hay Hall at Stillman, from its seat on the Heights, one can see over to the campus of the University of Alabama, where not that long ago George Wallace stood in another doorway. On election night in 2008, that same doorway saw a silent vigil as the results of the election became known. Late into the evening, in ones and twos, people silently walked through the famous door and into the ruined and decaying basketball arena of Foster's Auditorium, waiting there for the news of Barack Obama's election as president to be official.

Earlier that day, I went to vote in my suit and tie. I waited for hours in the heat of Alabama to approach the table with the ladies dressed to the nines. Everyone was dressed up, fanning with the paper fans provided by the candidates. It was as quiet as a white church. The sound of the markers pulling through the names on the roll. The tractor-fed sheets of the roll, sheet after sheet, yellow yellow. The ladies glowed as they worked in the close heat. I thanked them when they handed me the ballot and the pen to bubble in the empty O. I slipped my ballot into the scanning machine and brought the pen back to them. I thanked the ladies at my table, M to O, and in unison in that hushed and solemn room, they told me I was welcome.

The Ice-Mulched Breast of the New World

I kid and say that I now live in Alabama, below the bug line. I kid but that line is real. Environmentally I live south of a climate boundary where the mean annual temperature does not fall to the level cold enough to kill insects. In January crickets sing and peepers peep. One can discover in the South the homes of displaced Midwesterners like me who miss the chance, in the land of rhododendron and azalea, to grow peonies below the bug line. It is not that it gets too hot in the summer growing season to stifle the peony, but that it does not get cold enough, as the crown of the plant needs to freeze over the winter in order to thrive. I like to tour through town, looking for the telltale mounds of ice in a lawn, in a border, for a Midwesterner mulching a bed with ice, attempting to start a stand of peonies.

Back to critical lenses to gauge how we mean to mean. I am surprised still that the old regionalism has not gained new traction in the rhetoric and rubrics of the discourse of postcolonial theory. It is the end of winter in Tuscaloosa, and at the University of Alabama we are finishing up a search for a postcolonial specialist. Among the finalists was a scholar from Europe whose work centered on Haiti. He addressed the colony's relationship to France, examining colonial literature, concentrating on the social discourse between the colonizer and the colonized. His work focused on how that discourse shaped and produced the literature, subjectivity, and otherness. This candidate, though, was rejected, as his future work concerned the relationship between England and its colony of Georgia. My colleagues passed over the candidate on the grounds that we already had our expert in Southern literature.

Still, at the end of *Gatsby*, even as the book tries hard to be the American novel, Nick Caraway says it is about the West, the Midwest. Remember Sinclair Lewis's *Main Street*? I'm sure you don't. Might it be reread as a reversal of power positions, an attempt to manufacture a cultural world located outside the New Yorkish empire, with subject matter itself that worries a subaltern inferiority and parochial despair?

Postpostcards from the Cracker Barrel

In Lebanon, Tennessee, headquarters of the successful theme restaurant Cracker Barrel, there is a mock restaurant used by teams of interior decorators who meticulously plan the tableau of every single location, arrange the elements for each new store (old feed-lot signs, wagon wheels, pitchforks, tintypes, etc.) in a way that looks "right" to them. They then make a photographic plan for where the objects should go and send it off with those objects to the new location for final deployment. The design seems saturated in placeness, placefulness and those other elements of place—timelessness and timefulness. But the constructed environment's design elements do not obey any real (what is "real," in any case?) historical or geographical order. The Cracker Barrel as a place reads in general as a General Store, an anywhere-in-America mercantile of anytime in the last two centuries. The stove and fireplace and peaked roof are indicative of a Vermont country store, while the porch with rocking chairs bespeaks Southernness. The eponymous cracker barrel is the universal fountain of commonness, not specificity.

The country-store side of the property is crowded with merchandise that emanates vibes of localness, familyness, and small-batchness, while the abundant and artfully arranged junkiness of overstockage of stuff gives one the sense of possibility, of finding the ordinary out of the ordinary, the remembered in the long forgotten. You are an archeologist sifting through the detritus of a vaguely agrarian preindustrialized-capital world. You are a consumer of the preconsumer economy. A place before there was the notion of place. Of course this place is so consciously not a specific place—but it's certainly a "place" found between the signposts of quotes. It has all the details of place but not the particulars of any one place. I think of it as a caddis fly larva of place, attaching to its adhesive carapace the interesting stuff other places have sloughed off, lost as well as imported. Most of the merchandise is imported from China, where to this date Cracker Barrel has no retail outlet. The grand effect is not that you are in Tuscaloosa, Alabama, or Fort Wayne, Indiana (places now drained of their specific peculiarities), but that you are in a place that calls itself Place, the place of place. One would think that such a place—one that displays and merchandises the detritus of place—would have postcards to sell, postcards displayed for no other reason than to reinforce the Cracker Barrel's camouflage as the kind of shop that would have postcards. But, no, the stores do not have even a prop spinner of generic postcards advertising the locations of different Cracker Barrels. Cracker Barrel carries no postcards, and especially not cards illustrating the town it inhabits. One does not need to inform folks back home of the other places one has visited when back home, now, is exactly as exotic and different as the exotic and different places one visits. No need to write "Wish you were here" when the wish, through the complete draining of the swamp of place, has been granted. Here, now is everywhere. And you find yourself in the middle of it.

I-65

It takes a whole day, thirteen, fourteen hours, to drive from Tuscaloosa, Alabama, to Fort Wayne, Indiana. The first hour of the trip is spent on I-20/59 and the last two hours on I-69, but most of the time, a good ten hours, will be spent on I-65. Not all of that is driving, of course. I take breaks, fill the tank twice. There is always road construction. In the last fifteen years, I have made this trip, maybe, forty times, not all of them round trips. Over the years, I have bought three cars in Indiana (Alabama has binding arbitration rules and no lemon law) and driven the highway one-way. I am from Fort Wayne, and my family lives there still. There have been birthday trips, hospitalizations, Thanksgivings, deaths. Six hundred and sixty miles, my door to my parents' door, four hundred and eighty of those on I-65.

The purpose of today's drive is unlike any other. I am driving to Fort Wayne to see a play, *Alive and Dead in Indiana*. I didn't write the play. Doug Long adapted my stories. The Fort Wayne Civic Theater is staging the play in its Playwright Festival, and my parents are excited as there are characters in the play named Michael Martone's Mother and Michael Martone's Father. Doug calls it a chamber theater piece. Not much narrative in the series of vignettes. The narrative point of view has pivoted to a character named Michael Martone who will do a lot of talking directly to the audience, an audience (if I make it) that will include me, Michael Martone.

Most of the vignettes, I will soon discover, have to do with cars and driving. James Dean in a car. Colonel Sanders touring. Building cars in Fort Wayne. The race at Indianapolis. I will be surprised that I have written so much on the subject. I guess I think about driving when I am driving. Or perhaps I think about thinking about driving when I am driving and then, later, I write about it.

But that is a ways away for now. I am traveling with my wife, Theresa, and my son, Nick. We are in a rental car, a gold Toyota Camry with thirty-five thousand and some miles.

You enter onto I-65 in downtown Birmingham at a place known as Malfunction Junction, the exit ramp from I-20/59 descending from overhead into the northbound passing lane of I-65 at a point where it leans into an ascending grade, the semis over your right shoulder down-shifting with laboring cars speeding by the stalling trucks into a truncated, quickly narrowing acceleration lane, attempting to merge into a three-laned occluded pack of very grumpy and territorially sensitive vehicles. Nick's head is in the way. He is reading one of the George R. R. Martin books on his Kindle. It is at this moment too that the NPR station in Tuscaloosa gets swallowed up in distant wooded static, and Theresa seeks the burbling Birmingham feed. The highway is elevated here, the concrete flexing, booming at the seams, and here is at the tail end of the Appalachian chain, so we are climbing into some clear-channel green foothills all around, the statue of Vulcan on Red Mountain in the rearview, going 80 in a 65-mile per-hour zone.

I-65 is an archipelago of such interchanges, three more islands in the chain—Nashville, Louisville, Indianapolis—each with its own multilaned double helixes, mutations of interchanges, beltways, loops, bypasses. Occasions of orchestrated panic—the slalom across six lanes in Nashville as I-24 unbraids from I-65, the hairpin turn onto the bridge over the Ohio with the hilarious hieroglyphic warning diamond of a truck rolling over, the very unlucky cloverleaf on the south side of Prozac-enriched Indianapolis.

But most of the time will be spent relentlessly driving, driving, driving. Cruise control fools you into thinking you can think, find the groove in the grooved highway.

Kentucky seems close to triple-laning its whole stretch of I-65. Over the years, I've crept through the cautious summers of construction there. Blast zones, disappearing shoulders, detours, paved and Jersey-bermed medium strips. This trip there is work around the Cave and the Lincoln Birthplace exits near where the giant T-Rex points, with its tiny hands, to the sign that says I have missed Dinosaur World.

Where was I?

I was writing about grooves and thinking about the grooved roadbed, the endless corduroy fabric of it on the three lanes slouching into Louisville, microgutters to squeegee the rainwater away and, when dry, set up, at a certain speed, a humming harmonic of Radiohead on the radio.

We packed no snacks in order to force ourselves to stop every couple of hours. At Athens, a Starbucks. In winter, I'd get a hot chocolate, but instead, I grab a can of Sun Drop, my current preferred caffeine delivery device. Theresa ratchets around the iPod. We have been listening to *Fresh Air* podcasts, interviews with the casts of *Porgy and Bess* and the writers of *The Book of Mormon*. Sendak, recently dead. Terry mashes up all the interviews with him. He stopped signing his books for children, he says, because it was a terrifying experience for children—this strange stranger marking up a book your parents told you you can't write in.

We rush through the haze of electromagnetic soup we live in—cell towers everywhere. On the previous trip, a call caught up to us informing me that, Janine, my high school girlfriend, had died. I spent the long cedar-lined trip through southern Tennessee, detailing to Nick, in high school then, my own high school journey. That too, took place in cars, driving. Field trips, speech meets, mindless cruising, dating, driving into drive-ins.

So many days in automobiles. I move through the familiar, the bland, the planned and maintained corridors of normal. Interstated. Innerstated. Sated. Here is what I look forward too as I I-65:

The railroad siding near Vinemont, Alabama, seen from an overpass, where a little pusher locomotive rests, waiting to help the next freight train over Sand Mountain.

The Saturn Five rocket hulk dwarfing the welcome center.

The racking and walking horse signs.

The Polk Hotel billboard.

The spire of the Corvette Museum and the pilgrimage of Stingrays on the road. This trip I count five.

How soon it is, once in Indiana, for John Mellencamp to sing on the radio.

That massive yard of lawn ornaments for sale where I always say to myself I have to stop there on the way back.

The Bypass

The Johnny Appleseed Motel

Sixty years ago, after fleeing their wedding reception in the basement of Queen of Angels Church, my parents made their way, in a borrowed car, to the Johnny Appleseed Motel on the Bypass to spend their first night together as husband and wife. They were on their way up U.S. Highway 30 to Chicago for a honeymoon weekend at the Palmer House. The diversion to the Johnny Appleseed (only a mile or two from the church) always seemed to me (when my parents recounted the events of the day on each subsequent anniversary) as a wild, spontaneous act of passion. They couldn't help themselves. They helped themselves. They couldn't even make it out of town, could only launch themselves far enough to attain this shallow suborbital arch around their city, the Bypass, before reentry, before splashdown.

The motel was one of the first things built on the new Bypass, a road cobbled together into a sweeping curve, sine and cosine, from existing axes of township roads. One road was named California, and that name still survives today as a remnant, a residue, a notion of the romance of the open road. The Bypass bent the old roads to its will; a bent bow flexed from east of Fort Wayne then, to the north, then north by northwest, crazy that way.

The Johnny Appleseed Motel had that postwar rambling ranch footprint, a row house made out of the older model motor court, free-standing detached cabins all squashed together in a long, narrow barrack of adjacent rooms. Of course, there were yellow bug-lights illuminating the dozen doors, and its simple lean-to roof was outlined with one endless tube of red neon, perhaps sputtering in places. It was August and hot and this was before central air conditioning, even before built-in window units. The only ventilation was the single sashed window next to the screened door. There was a sign too, I imagine, the neon curved to outline the profile of the folk hero, the eccentric identifiable cook pot perched on his head. And there must have been that beckoning "vacancy" sign sparking in the office window, the vacuumed absence of the unlit invisible "no" not there.

Why not? Why not stop? The convenience of the Bypass was not the conveyance after all, not the route of the journey but the journey's end.

They must have tumbled into the room exhausted, excited. The dramatic shadows of the 1950s, projected from the light of the motel's sign (the illuminated silhouette of the folk hero, the cook pot helmet—red-hot and glowing on his head) painted the room with the film noir stripes of the Venetian blinds that contoured objects in the dim light with strips of romantic camouflage traced in an organic cling of French curves.

Every time we would pass the ruins of the place years later, my parents always said they just slept. "We just slept." The building had gone to seed, its paint peeled and its lighting dimmed and broken. The Johnny Appleseed had gone to seed. The motel had then turned into rented by the week apartments, leased to tenants who seemed partial to motorcycles and muscle cars. Big chromed hogs herded in the crushed stone dust of the parking lot.

My parents left early the next morning to begin their honeymoon in earnest, anxious to make it quickly to Chicago. There, they would discover, unknown to them on their way up the Lincoln Highway, a telegram waited for them at the Palmer House. My mother's grandfather had suffered a stroke the night before after coming home from the wedding, had been in the hospital all that night my parents were at the Johnny Appleseed Motel, unreachable, incommunicado, on the road somewhere. My parents never checked in at the Palmer House but drove right back to Fort Wayne; the night in the motel would have to do for a honeymoon.

Now, sixty years later, the Johnny Appleseed Motel is gone. In its place a TCS store parking lot, I think. Without the actual building I get confused about just where it stood, on which side of the single railroad track intersecting the Bypass, the spur line heading north to Grand Rapids.

Look quickly as you speed by on the Bypass, out over the shimmering desert expanse of the Coliseum parking lot, there in the distance on the little rise beneath the arbor of high-tension wires strung from the dam on the St. Joe River, is the grave of Johnny Appleseed. Of course, the owners of my parents' bower of bliss, the Johnny Appleseed Motel, needed a name and cleverly landed on Johnny Appleseed, who also slept here, down the road.

Growing up in his resting place, I vaguely recall the protracted legal wrangling with Leominster, Massachusetts, John Chapman's birthplace, over the body's final disposition. Fort Wayne seems to have won. The little precinct is maintained and has been spruced up a bit with flowering crabapple trees. There is an annual festival now, flea market booths and fried dough stands blooming over one long weekend in the parking lot below.

All that came later. I found myself at the grave one April forty years ago when I was in high school, with a girl, a classmate. We climbed the hill and rested against the fence enclosing the grave of Johnny Appleseed and watched the cars and trucks speed by on the Bypass in the distance. We had walked there from Shoaff Park, north beyond the Bypass, where we had arranged to meet that morning. Our parents, unaware of our conspiracy, had dropped us off separately at the wowo Kite Fly. We were so clever. We half-heartedly watched kites fly, our hearts racing with the adrenaline of young love. Looking for an excuse to be together longer, we decided to walk home, a good hike, instead of calling our parents for rides.

Was it a long walk? I didn't notice. We made it to the gravesite, to the grassy hill, deserted, neglected, a modest distance from the ceaseless traffic on the horizon. We kissed, trying it out, ignoring the creepier aspects of the setting, endowing the place with all the romance we could muster. That kiss seemed to be over in an instant, and it seemed to last forever. I remember thinking that I would one day write a poem about this moment, maybe write several innocent poems to commemorate it. Instead I'll write this: On the Bypass the trucks downshifted on the grade leading to the bridge over the river. The traffic made a steady bee-like hum and buzz, an ambient backdrop to this sentimental urban pastoral.

The Backyard

From the house where my parents lived, in a subdivision called New Kirkwood Park, they could see the Bypass. There it is out their back windows beyond their backyard and on the other side of a large expanse of lawn, part of an office park that has always, it seems, been there with its scattered arrangement of a few modern buildings and landscaped lake, fountain, and meadow.

This stretch of the Bypass is an odd leg on the route. It stands in stark contrast to the rest of the road, the more typical strip developments, a repeating pattern of constantly churning chain store façades and franchises interspersed with the parking lot permutations.

Years ago, my parents organized with their neighbors to prevent Lowe's from buying up this seemingly bucolic property in their backyards. Lowe's wanted to construct another hardware supercenter with its more than ample parking lot. My mother learned in the process that she was now a NIMBY. She ignored the negative connotation of the acronym—the implied hypocrisy of the NIMBY who only becomes radicalized when the transgression happens in one's own backyard. Mom, proudly, adopted the identity. She took the message of Not In My Backyard unironically. Instead of their property expanding gracefully into the reaches of what had been an insurance company's conspicuous consumption of lawn, they would now be backed up against massive loading docks blazing with sodium security lights and the sneezing airbrakes of trucks.

I was amazed they won. Lowe's located farther back down the Bypass, bulldozing, I believe, a church. It butts up against only other business properties—gas stations, fast food outlets, pharmacies—who don't mind what sprouts in their backyards, who, in fact, welcome such an infestation explained by the market theory of clustering.

I was even more amazed that the green sweep of the park survived as long as it did to be so recently threatened. The collapse of the insurance company and the purchase by Chicago's Beatrice Foods of the local meatpacker, Eckrich, who also maintained an understated headquarters building in the park, had left the property ripe for the picking.

The huge flock of Canada geese still grazed the lawn beneath the willows around the lake with its fountain that, even when the buildings sat empty, continued to spout, its plume posting rainbows occasionally in the refracted air. For a long time, it seemed, the geese were the only inhabitants of the place. They would find their way over to my parents' backyard in search of the greener pasture. They milled about there, animated lawn ornaments.

Of course, driving out Lowe's did not save the park's pristine nature for long. The very public squabble had marked the space as prime real estate, perhaps the only undeveloped lot left on the Bypass. Sensing this pressure, my parents and their neighborhood allies compromised with the relentless developers. Instead of building a big retail property, smaller vest-pocket boutique concerns were constructed. The land was subdivided again and again. There is now an assisted living center that looks like a Victorian mansion in the corner of the Bypass and Hobson. Behind it, there is a boxy credit union branch. And behind it, a small clinic specializing in outpatient endoscopy nestles next to my parents' next-door neighbors' back fence. The doctors who run the clinic have now just broken ground on an adjoining office building. The backhoes are excavating along the edge of my parents' property. Soon a tasteful two-story façade will wall away the vista, drop a curtain of bricks out back.

For a little while longer my parents still were taken in by the illusion of their vast holdings. Their back lawn extended forever. Or it expanded for at least as long as a few football fields toward the Bypass in the distance. Even after the new building was finished, they were still able to celebrate the Fourth of July in their traditional manner. They held a neighborhood party out on the common ground.

The gaggle of geese is curiously intent following the badminton shuttlecock. The birds' heads track the flight of the birdie. Bocce balls bowl at their webbed feet. My parents set up the theater of lawn chairs to face the impending fireworks display. The rockets will be launched from the Memorial Coliseum farther west down the Bypass. Everyone sits and watches the sun sink. At their backs the black night creeps up on them from the east, moving like a gaggle of traffic along the bottleneck of the Bypass behind them.

Even though it is a holiday, there seems to be some activity in the original buildings of the office park, the buildings that once housed the headquarters of the butcher and the insurer. The big air conditioning units come on, their fans throbbing and whirring. I think one of the new tenants is a unit of the Postal Service. Inside the modernist box of a building, behind the smoked glass windows, hundreds of clerks sit in cubicles before video monitors. On the screens are pictures of letters, their addresses obscure, hard to read, defaced, smudged. The actual letters could be in any post office. Their images are being fed to this station in Fort Wayne. These letters are undeliverable, can't be read by the automated scanning machines of the local branches. The dead letters are shipped virtually to my parents' backyard. The clerks decode and decipher. The office works night and day and even on holidays. Out on the lawn, we have all settled in for the fireworks. We eagerly anticipate the annual ritual of intricate patterns, the thump of distant mortars, and the window-rattling booms of the grand finale. Traffic pulses east and west on the Bypass in the distance. Behind their glass walls, the postal clerks passively press on. They decide, route letters and packages remotely, never touching the mail. Touching a few buttons, they determine where in the world each piece of it should go. And then it goes.

Happy Meals

I was born in 1955, the same year as the opening of Disneyland, the commencement of the Interstate Highway system, and the founding of McDonald's. I think of these chiming inaugurations as a kind of chord, a harmonic of what was going to (of what actually did) happen in my lifetime. Roads and cars and places to drive cars to. I was to spend a lot of time in cars. I still spend a lot of time in cars.

The first car I remember riding around in was born in 1956. It was a two-door copper-and-cream Bel Air my father bought secondhand from Beuter Chevrolet. It came equipped with a flimsy car seat, a frame of chrome tubing and plaid patterned vinyl. The car seat had a plastic steering wheel with a button horn my younger brother continually honked. The contraption was secured by two tube crooks that hooked over the seat, held in precarious place by gravity.

Gravity allowed the carhop at Gardner's on Jefferson downtown to affix her tray to the Chevy's slightly rolled-up driver-side window. My younger brother was strapped (the strap was a ribbon width of elastic cinched by a buckle with teeth) in the car seat. My mother used the popped-open door of the glove compartment as a little table for the fries and frosties. I had the back seat to myself, and my father handed me my burger and malt. I set my table on the upholstered shelf behind the backseat, the placemat marked by the perforations of the hidden radio speaker. I bellied up to this bar, nursed my shake while watching through the picture window before me the hubbub across the street at the wedding-cake-shaped Greyhound station.

It wasn't long before I tipped over my drink, the sludgy liquid draining into the speaker ports. My father, out of the car immediately, had the trunk lid up, tried to staunch the dripping leak, sopping up the puddle with a thousand paper napkins the carhop trundled out to him. I could see him through the crack. My brother wailed, craned in his seat, unable to see what was going on behind him. Mother held her drink and my father's drink and balanced his twice-bitten sandwich on the rolled lips of the paper cups, the torn bits of my brother's sandwich on her lap.

How strange this wasn't strange, this eating in the car. I had been born in this saddle it seems, borne by the Bel Air. It wasn't simply that we drove to places where we would eat but that we ate so many meals right in the car we drove. The armrests were designed precisely, it appeared, to accommodate a bag of fries wedged in the little pocket of the handle. After the accident of the ledge, I employed the carpeted hump of the driveshaft housing on the floor as my table, spreading out the place setting of paper wrapping, garnished with the blob of ketchup for dipping. We traveled the city, driving from drive-in to drive-in (this was before drive-thrus), our passenger compartment converting to our dining nook as Dad dropped the bags on the carving board of the front seat.

To reach the McDonald's on the Bypass took us hours, it seemed, to make the trip. Out State past the shopping center where Keltsch Pharmacy had a soda fountain and a lunch counter, out Wells past the Sol Wood home for wayward boys, out to the Bypass at its junction with Indiana 3, then headed east.

The McDonald's looked a little like the bus station, all streamlined organic and skinned with its tooth-tinted tile. This was the old-style shack, not the current mansard-roofed walk-in but the walk-up lean-to with its parabolic flying buttresses of neon loopily looping overhead.

I liked McDonald's right away. From certain angles I could get those arches to add up to the architecture of my initials. It looked like the whole building was suspended from that M, swinging on the swing set cantilevering above us as we rolled into the parking lot, orbited, looked for a spot to set up shop.

The Bypass had only recently opened up. Across the road was a large copse of trees and behind us the terrain sloped away into farm fields and pastures inhabited by curious cud-chewing cattle that congregated into lumpy undulating hummocks of fur at the fence. The cars herded together in the blacktop parking lot. Occasionally, a "ponk" of a car horn sounded as its occupant reached for the next hamburger or handed out the fries.

As we ate, the cattle watched us eat. I was old enough to appreciate the irony of this. After dinner we could get out of the car and ease up to their bumpy huddles. The cattle started, huffed, and shuffled off only to reconfigure in the distance, nonchalantly drift back toward us, sniffing, their cowed cow eyes eyeing us.

Then one day, trampoline pits appeared like mushrooms in the lot next to the McDonald's. Each trampoline was suspended at ground level over a grave-size pit so that the hurtling inertia of the descending jumpers depressed the trampoline below ground and then, rebounding, popped up again to the grade while flinging the jumpers who hurtled upward again, suspended, then fell. There must have been several dozen such pits, gridded into a neat pattern, the walkways between them landscaped with white sparkling gravel.

In the car with our meals, we ate in silence and watched the oscillations, up and down and up and down. The more adventurous performers slowly twisted, skewed, flipped through their weightless contortions as they rose. Others, as they plummeted, calmly sat down into the smack of the canvas and sank, a cannonball into a pool, only to be shot out again, recoiled projectiles up into the blue sky. Dozens of people, adults and kids, floated suspended, falling upward, sank, leaping, always hitting the ground, it seemed, and then going lower as if planted to the waist, then springing, full-bodied bodies, up, up, and up.

My father wouldn't let me go over to the pits, especially after the cheese-burgers and orange drink. McDonald's then dispensed root beer from a real-looking barrel and orange drink from a fountain that could have been a converted washing machine that sprayed the soda in sheets inside a big glass ball. That dramatic agitation illustrated for my father the digestive stress young stomachs were under as they percolated in the neighboring pits. And, yes, occasionally, a flyer next door would, um, "lose" his stomach, the contents of which took flight before us. I watched closely, trying to guess as I chewed, who, of the current performers, seemed ripe.

Just as quickly the pits were gone, the whispered rumor of one too many participants having veered off on faulty trajectories, suffered unfortunate reentries, splashed down on the crushed quartz. This was the sixties, and all metaphors could be couched in space. And the little launching pads did give way to another kind of space.

We ate our last meals at that McDonald's sitting in the car watching the massive yellow graders, distorted Dr. Seuss contraptions, scrape away the farm fields, clear the copse, and level the pastures. I remember the tiny men in the distance perched above the growling engines protected from the elements only by these absurdly little parasols. The machines hauled behind a big bucket wagon, dragging the gouging scraper and a conveyor conveying the dirt to the gaping hopper.

Our entertainment was not vertical now, but horizontal comings and goings. Back and forth the graders ground down the ground, packed it, filled it, leveled it.

In our car, my family ate. We didn't know it then but this new expanding horizon would become the parking lots of the mall across the Bypass, the Kmart behind the McDonald's. We would eat a meal and watch them work. The leveled ground was sealed and paved. We watched from our parking place as we ate. We watched right up until the day the asphalt was painted with its fishbone pattern of empty, waiting spaces and the new parking lot connected seamlessly to the one in which we were parked watching.

Gravely

I have a picture of my mother and father sitting on their gravestone. The granite slab is one of those modern flat numbers, contoured to the ground meant not to interrupt, with a vertical spire or bulky tablet, the uninterrupted view of the green sward of the cemetery. The meadow is more easily maintained without the hodgepodge of Victorian monuments or copses of trees found in the older plots. The one stone is big enough to record all the vital statistics for both of them, side by side. They are happy, laughing, sitting on their gravestone. They have finished this part of their ending, the final arrangements arranged. Some of the mystery of their future ending has been resolved. I like knowing that back then, thirty years ago, they were thoroughly optimistic when they purchased the stone. They didn't have the 19 carved in anticipation of their death's date but tempted fate and affixed 20 instead.

They are smiling at the camera, laughing really. The picture was taken soon after the marker was installed. They look so young. They are quite conscious they have a whole new life in front of them, having just retired. The stone is in a new section of the cemetery, a block from where Lake Avenue crosses the Bypass. When I visit home, we sometimes drive out the Bypass to the cemetery to visit the grave. Often we'll see a long line of cars, their lights on and the little magnetic flags attached to the hood, coast by, arching toward one of the cemeteries, stalling traffic, a kind of rolling roadblock backing up the highway. The trees and the shrubbery have grown up, spread out. New graves and gravesites have extended the grounds farther east toward the bowling alley and the Bypass. Many more graves are now occupied, the closing numbers chipped freshly into the sparkling marbles or granites.

Follow Lake back out to the Bypass. Now a Home Depot occupies the site of what once was the Golden Corral, a cheap family steakhouse restaurant where you stood in line to order your slab of meat and were given a plastic number representing the cut in a color that represented its doneness. The help was done up in cowboy duds, red-checked shirts and bolo ties, delivering your rib eye, medium well, with a brain-like baked potato on its own plate and another plate for the Texas toast, a whole loaf of bread disguised as a one thick slice, all of it carried to your table on an orange tray the size and shape of a manhole cover.

Either before it was The Golden Corral or after it was the Golden Corral, the restaurant was a pancake place with a menu of designer pancakes, waffles, and crepes. I liked the lazy Susan in the center of each table where the dozen syrup cruets were stored in several tiers in identical glass bottles that differed only in their shades of infused fruits and maple extracts, blues to blacks and ambers turning smoky. I turned them slowly. A traffic of syrups, a berry-go-round. It was there, after my first communion at Queen of Angels earlier that morning, that the whole family converged for breakfast. I was still in my official outfit—white shirt, blue blazer, and navy pants. The matching blue tie was still clipped on the too-tight collar.

You should see my first communion picture. I look so serious, even my mouth is one determined straight poignant line, my eyes pensive, plaintive. I look, well, beatific, holy even. I could be a staring icon. The reality was that I hurt like hell. The week before the ceremony a brace of orthodontic retainers had been applied to my unruly teeth and all of them ached. Truth be told, my whole mouth ached—gums, tongue, roof, cheeks, lips, even the uvula, I imagine. The picture doesn't document the communion with the divine but a very worldly vanity. The next week, I would faint at the altar rail at morning mass, a result of my new regimen of communion fasting aggravated by the secular fast imposed by the appliance in my head. The nuns mistook my swoon for a kind of sacred possession, and I let them think of me as one so possessed.

I have forgotten the breakfast that Sunday. What combination of batter and filling did I order and not eat? What kind of fruit flavor had been drizzled over the powdered sugared waffles, the butter glazed silver dollars? I do remember that this morning is the last memory of my grandmother, my father's mother, and it was made there on the Bypass. She ended up in Fort Wayne after an arranged marriage, arriving from Italy to wed my Grandpa Moosh. Moosh worked nights as a janitor at the Hotel Indiana, and so in the days, when I saw him, he always sported a fresh stubble. "Moosha, moosh," he would say, taking my hand in his and sanding his cheeks with my fingers. "Moosha, moosh." The family story is that Grandpa got on the train in New York City after fleeing the old country's influenza, heading for Chicago, getting off a few stops early in Fort Wayne, thinking it was Chicago, staying when he found out. Too much trouble to move again.

Grandma wore a dark dress with a print of tiny flowers. She wore a hat with a net veil and white gloves and ate very little, in sympathy with my pathetic nibbling. The Lazy Susan spun. The whole family sampled the syrups. Around and around, the bottles, with their curved handles and thumb-operated trigger that slid the trapdoor spout, dripped dew down their sides. But it was impossible to open my mouth. That morning's performance had exhausted me, the Host coming in for a landing on my throbbing tongue. And there across the table, my grandmother not eating too, probably too ill to eat, looked at me, murmured very syrupy words in Italian. "Eat," she probably said, "eat."

My parents take the Bypass out to visit the graves of their parents. They are in the Catholic Cemetery. The Bypass is a convenient way to get there. Once the cemetery was on the edge of town but now it is adjacent to the bowling lanes. The Home Depot is across the street where once the Golden Corral had been, then the pancake house, then a Korean church. And back across the Bypass and across Lake from the cemetery is a photographer's studio where I sat for my high school graduation portrait. I had, as they say, my whole life ahead of me. I was wearing a polyester coat and tie. I was able to smile, and you can see my expensively corrected teeth. After the sitting, I pulled out of the parking lot, glancing across the street through the wrought-iron fence at the rolling meadow of graves. I turned left to go back to the Bypass intersection. The traffic there was backed up, a parking lot. Six lanes of stalled cars and trucks. It was quitting time at the factories on the east side. The next shift was starting in the same factories. People were going home or going to work. Or they were just going, just going to go. I slowly worked my way into a seam in the jam and then just sat. All of us, now, were going nowhere, fast.

Donuts

The Bypass isn't a beltway. It doesn't orbit, completely, Fort Wayne. It's not like that raceway, 465, haloing Indianapolis, not like any of the 4-something numbered loops, looping major cities coast to coast. No, the Bypass is more a blister, bubbling out on the city's north side. It transcribes, in its outline, the silhouette of the sun just rising above or just setting below the horizon line. An omega. An upended U. It traces an arch, a semicircle, and it implies, in the sweeping gesture it makes, the other missing half, its submerged tropic scallop turning back on itself.

I love the word "Quonset." I really didn't know how much I liked the word "Quonset" until I published my first book of stories and the editor pointed out, in the style sheet she produced to standardize her corrections, my fondness of the word "Quonset." She found that I had used it in every one of my stories. I hadn't realized. And look, the fondness continues. I used "Quonset" here. I love the Quonset hut as well, the prefabricated building of arcing corrugated steel that looks like a half-buried pipe, the walls turning into the roof and then back into walls again. I have even been to visit the spit of land in Rhode Island, Quonset Point, jutting out into Narragansett Bay, where the huts were invented for use during the Second World War.

As long as I can remember there has been a Quonset hut on the Bypass, a relic of the war, no doubt. They were sold as surplus. A hundred bucks bought you a building. I love that Falkner Tire, the owner of the Quonset there where Wells Street empties into the Bypass, has painted the crescent of the flat metal end with the image of a giant tire, white-walled and mag-wheeled, "Hub Cap Express" arching overall. Architects call such building "ducks," a mimetic structure made to look like the merchandise for sale within, after the duck-shaped building on Long Island selling Long Island duck. No doubt Falkner Tires sells tires even though this graphic wheel seems stuck in the mud.

But I like the chiming association the advertisement invokes. Behind the decorated Quonset are the metal boxes of trailers and mobile homes moored in an ancient park round back. And I remember, or I want to remember, that the lanes and alleyways running through the court were lined with half-buried whitewashed tires, undulating serpents snaking along the edges of the trailer skirts, the insulating hay bales, and the cinderblock supports.

Hard by the trailers, the Speed Way Café was open all hours, where I imagine once patrons sank their cake sinkers in black black coffee. The Speed Way Café, "Booze and Chow" its understated subheading promotion beneath its name, took that name from an actual stock car speedway a block east, barely visible in my memory and all but invisible today, its ruins plowed under and paved over by flag-flying car dealerships selling actual cars in stock. All that's left is the road sign radiating off the Bypass and the shell of the closed tavern still labeled Speedway Café. Look at the O's in "Booze and Chow." Don't they seem to lean to the right? Aren't they slightly elliptical as if they were wheels in motion, biting in with great torque and traction? A cartoon rendition of speed, of going nowhere fast.

On the other side of Indiana 3, next to Hall's Hollywood, the Roller Dome still hosts its spinning, its own compliment of O's. "Roller Dome." The name rode on the ball bearings of assonance, interjections of delight. Oh! Oh! Oh! Not a dome so much as a pagoda-like pavilion elongated and curved at the Bypass end. Inside the rectangular ring of wood grooved with its endless circulating skaters, each on a pair of the four-wheeled version, no in-line blades, the analog of the cars that bought them there, that drove up to the drive-in next door, whose hops, I suppose, once wore the same footwear to propel them from car to car, orbiting the lot as the headlights flashed on and off. While back in the Dome the management hung a mirrored disco ball that rotated with the music, wheeled within the wheeling wheel of the skaters, light playing off the sphere and dancing over the polyester, the sequins, the sunglasses worn indoors.

The Gerber Haus, a motel and restaurant farther east, was lodged in the Bermuda Triangle formed by the confluence of Parnell and Clinton with the Bypass. There, in its pool, I learned, or more accurately, didn't learn, how to swim. The daily lessons one summer found me pretending to lap the pool, but really I simply slid from one end to the other on my running dive's inertia. I somehow missed the lesson on breathing and never gathered that one should breathe out into the water while stroking. So when I turned my head out of the wake, I had to exhale first then gulp in a lungful of pool that would swamp me. It was bad enough the weekday mornings floundering at the Gerber Haus but my family frequented its restaurant on Sundays for brunch after church. But what was served there made up for going back.

The centerpiece of the meal was a donut. It was no ordinary donut but massive, as if inflated, plump, as large as a small animal brain. The crowning touch was that this donut came with its own hole—not the hole hole but the solid kind, a perfect sphere of dough teed up on the dimple where it had been punched out from the dough before the frying. The effect was stunning, a tiered conglomeration of curving terraces, the drizzle of icing dripping down, pooling, spilling, glazing everything, a Mobius of milky melted sugar. To eat it, you had to dissemble the components, hole from donut, as if you were disjointing a joint with frosting cartilage—ball from socket.

What was her name, the woman who invented this marriage of cruller and wedding cake? She ran the show at the Gerber Haus. I reeked of chlorine and stink-eyed the pool out back as I deconstructed my donut, my hands sticky with the business. I remember our hostess made the rounds, went from table to table. I remember her goggle glasses and that her hands, cupped and curled, seemed arthritic, lame. Perhaps they were even locked in some kind of brace. Am I remembering correctly? I recall thinking then that the crippled hands, the myopic eyes were no doubt the result of an unfortunate bakery accident, a donut experiment gone horribly wrong. The donut before me, resisting my assaults, did seem to defy the laws of physics as I then understood them. But even then, things in motion tended to stay in motion. And space, it was demonstrated on the plate before me, could be curved and warped. Time had always arched and stalled and started up again and then came back around to return over the same ground.

Sometime after the Gerber Haus closed, its pool was filled in for a parking lot of a Lincoln-Mercury dealer. Now the cars are long gone, replaced by a thrift store where I bought a secondhand topcoat before heading off to college. The nameless chef (what was her name?) moved to the Four Winds, another motel on the Bypass down beyond the Roller Dome and the Hub Cap Express and the Booze and Chow, where she continued to concoct her crazed donuts until the day, one day, I forget which one, I forgot to remember she was there until this moment now.

Far Out

The coolest spot in the world was out near the Bypass. On those hot summer nights, when sitting as still as you could with the breathless breeze becalmed on the screened-in porch, the iced drinks sweating in the jewel-toned anodized aluminum tumblers as the spiraling fireflies jitterbugged and the cicadas, organic thermostats, cranked up their feverish caterwauling, and you couldn't keep from steaming and sweating, your father would say, "Let's go." And you went. Launched, blasting off in the molten lozenge oven of the all-day-long-cooped-up coupe of a car capsule, the Oldsmobile rocketed out to the edge of the overheated universe. Your mother always said that a night like that was "close." "It's close," she would say, but you were heading out, far out, the lot of you, past the city gates of the Gateway Shopping center, past the crystalline cylindrical synchronous orbiting satellite of Club O, past the dried-up canals of the old Venice restaurant, out, out, out, not to the Milky Way but to the Lincoln Way to rendezvous with that Jetsonesque space station known terrestrially as the Fort Myers Truck Stop, with all its mod organic organ-shaped facades and crazy pastel plastic flying buttresses, its tethered panting trucks, Kerouacian dinosaurs melting into bubbling tar pit pools of sodium vapor lights. It was as if your dad used the place to slingshot the whole kit and caboodle whiplashed and merging onto the holy radiating sweeping arch of the Bypass. He wanted speed to blow the heat away. Once on the homing beam of glowing fluorescent street stripes ignited by the setting sun, illuminated by the Rocket's brights, the craft stuttered into overdrive, its v8 knocking to beat all, all the little vent windows angled to ricochet the wind around the mad baroque Detroit dream dash, echoing a series of sonic boomlets through the car, the air all jazzed and jumping. This was just air, man, no conditioning, daddy-o, this moving air moving as you moved. Now you peeled your skin from the clear plastic adhesive wrapper installed, back on earth, by artisans plying their trade at Seat Cover Charlie's, making that long insane ripping sound in the oily thick ticking flickering American night. You were aimed at the other end of this galaxy, the end of the road splashdown that was the Saturn V starship, a ship-shaped burning red tower, hip on its pad, grim reaper ready, at the Harvester. Bells rang, horns honked, that little buzzy buzzer buzzed that came standard on the heap, razzing you when the analog needle of the speedometer crept into the red zone above seventy. There wasn't a stoplight for miles. You howled Ginsbergian, having never read the poem but completely inoculated and wired by the atmospheric beat of the current zeitgeist. You were cool and getting cooler. Or Dad juked and jived, swerved, and turned into the DQ lot and made you all freeze your frontal lobes care of the hallucinogenic concoction called a "slush" that came in otherworldly flavors that were simply colors you could taste—red, blue, green, yellow—liquid ice inhaled through microscopic straws you picked up on the fly while circling the lot and sucked the color out of the pale, graying ice granules, then out, out even farther to Smith Field, where you paced along with the tiny lights of the tiny balletic Piper Cubs and Cessnas doing touch-and-goes, settling down just up ahead, just out of reach, the prop wash in their wakes adding to the accumulated moving air you moved through, with lightning bugs steaming out of the cornfields and the strobe light on the rickety tower strobing, strobing as you zoomed by, brains frozen, planes circling overhead in lazy circles with insect-whirring engines pitched and pitching, and only the stars falling, the bugs sparking, and the dashboard lights illumining your primal primary conventional makeup in the convecting heat, leaping into the clear but congested sky. Then you found a flying saucer beached, stranded in a parking lot in some remote outpost of the Bypass. A crowd of sweltering earthbound Earthlings gathered at its spidery feet, all of you struck dumb by the band of flickering lights undulating along the silver edge, casting its own eclipsed shadow, a numb penumbra, on the dusty Fort Wayneian ground. On the top a clear plastic bubble cockpit was all lit up from the inside and a humanoid looked as if he were a prize that came in one of the plastic prize blisters dispensed by cranking a knob after inserting your nickel and turning real real real slow, looking like that and looking out at you, the sweaty civilians looking for any prize that would distract you from the heat that was clotting and coating your skin like a coat of molten coats, looking out, out into the vast endlessly infinite Fort Wayneian night. It was, alas, merely a roadside mirage, an attraction cobbled out of plywood and dayglow paint to attract you rubes to a nearby development Polaroiding the cornfields into fields of houses, houses holding more heat, that would soon enough subdivide the infinite space of the Tri-State Area into quarter-acre lots. The occupant in the cockpit, a mere kid like you, waited to take a turn to feel—once you climbed up into the belly of the beast—like you were the alien you always suspected you were, mistakenly implanted with this family of freaks, some comic mistake or joke as you baked beneath the plastic canopy to the point of swooning, dizzily taking the craft out for a spin, out spinning flying over this city not of fallen angels exactly more like a city of fallen Waynes you now saw as another mirage of shimmering light through the haze of the superheated exhaust of a million cruising cars and burning inert neon flashing signs, the streetlamps still shielded from World War Two when everyone believed that Fort Wayne was seventh on Hitler's bombing list, the finger-smudged Plexiglas of your very own blinking and nodding 1950s American dream. But you have been abducted by the aliens in your family and you are back in the backseat of the mothership slaloming back and forth up the Bypass past the Buckminster bubble of the golden geodesic dome of the People's Bank, now long gone, turned back into parking lots, looking when you gaze upon the dome for all the world like a world, a planet, rising out of the space-black jet-black tarmac like a quilted afterthought of the big bang. You know where you are headed now. Gravity has latched on to the car's grinning grill and your father is taking you to the coolest spot on earth over near Schaumberg Dells, a dip in the road as you approach the turn. Your family, you, you all have all your arms out the open windows, your hands acting as ailerons, slicing through the forgiving wind, flipping back and forth and up and down, searching between each molecule for a modicum of relief, the sweat evaporating instantly. And WOWO is on the radio, its fifty thousand watts hurling the local weather report to the dark side of the planet over and under the polar ice caps, and your Dad says, "Here it comes." And your Mom says "So close." And then the little interruption in the road and you can feel the tires peel from the pavement for a second, airborne and flying, the 8 knocking again, and in that second you feel that minute shift in the physics of thermodynamics, the infinite space between two points where the BTUs have all abandoned ship, the fires are out, the coolest cool spot in the overheated city, one of those unexplained wonders of nature, a precinct the sun forgot to ignite, and you are coasting through, the space time continuum all screwy. You are so cool, so close, so close to cool.

Old Pond

A Lesson Plan in Tweets

We now live in, move through an electromagnetic soup. We steep in this invisible stew. Weightless text all around. An atomistic atmosphere.

We hold these devices, these slim slabs of veneered plastic nestled in our palms. Effortlessly, these inert boxes suck up text. Osmotically.

We walk. We leave the classroom. We write on our handheld devices, mobile by definition. As we walk, I remind them to look. I re-mind them.

As we walk, we attempt to see the things we overlook each day as we walk to the classroom where this walk began. Time to under look, to see.

In Alabama, below the bug line, we go outside, exit the classroom, roam. The bug line? Insects do not freeze in winter. Crickets in January.

The university promotes itself, publishes pamphlets with pictures of professors and their classes on the great green lawn of the Quad. Lies.

Lies. We're alone, staked-out, the only squad on the Quad. We lay about, taking notice of other students, heads down, noses in their phones.

Tuscaloosa's also known as Druid City. It's all the oak trees. The campus is rife with old growth, boughs bare in winter, but not bare bare.

There, in the upper most reaches, clouds of leaves caught up in the branches. I ask, "Has everyone noticed those?" No? Green thought balloons.

We speculate. What could they be? Squirrels' nests? Last season's persistence? They've never noticed this green scribble on the scaly limbs.

They've noticed that they've never noticed this patch of leaves before. They walk beneath this canopy each day. That's the point as I point.

It's mistletoe. The kissing you've been missing, clueless as you understory daily. A parasite. Seeds planted by perching birds. "Dung twig."

Mistletoe. Now seen, we talk about the Golden Bough, connect it to the Druids (we are in Druid City, remember), the power of the puny plant.

The power to kill an oak, mistletoe. The tree's green soul. Druids used a gold sickle to harvest each solstice. In Alabama? A shotgun blast.

We stand, a copse of a class, point our phones up at the tree within a tree, take pictures, link, branching, root through the nets of roots.

I ask them why we think we can text and drive. They think about this. They think they shouldn't do it. They think they shouldn't think it.

I think, I say to them, we think we can text and drive because we seem to have an ability to filter, to sort, all the incoming stimulations.

It makes sense. Our senses would be overwhelmed, flooded by incoming information. Almost biological, this sense to notice this and not that.

I drive to here. It is routine. I think of the class. I listen to music. I remember something. Or not. There is nothing out of the ordinary.

I'm an automaton in an automobile. It's automatic, this drive. I can text. If something emerges. If there's an emergency. If there is an if.

We say we "focus" our attention because most of our experience is a blur. We also "pay" attention to something, a transaction that delivers.

See, most of the time, however, we delete without seeing. We edit. We gloss the world's goings-on. Vision is revised before we begin to see.

We see our seeing compromised, our algorithmic blindnesses, our machinations to sort the feed to, like Tweets in Twitter, trend. We trend.

Now, we get familiar with these Russians who confronted the all-too-familiar world made out of habit, making it a habit to get out of habit.

To create is not godlike, creating something out of nothing. To create is to reorder the things we know well in order to create new order.

Tonight at the cocktail party, you will talk about the Russians, the idea of defamiliarization, the active eye-opening intervention of art.

A cocktail party! An act of defamiliarization. I task the students to imagine my trivia hubbubed at a cocktail party's imaginary crossroads.

Back to the Russians. Writing works at dismantling that biological sense sieve sanding smooth the world. For both the reader and the writer.

The class is defamiliarization. Defamiliarize the classroom. Defamiliarize the class. Defamiliarize the campus. Defamiliarize their phones.

Defamiliarize the phones they carry, devolve those devices. Defamiliarize the writing they already do on their phones, the text and twitter.

the the the the the the the the the the the the the the the the the the the the the the the the the the the the the the the the the the the the

It happens, that moment, a word (say, "the") you write, you read goes south, goes sideways, goes strange when you no longer can make it mean.

I ask if they know what a combine is? What is a combine? One, two report a vague memory. A farm machine, they guess. Yes! But why "combine?"

Here's the way the mind works. When we harvested grain by hand we did so in 3 steps. 1st, we cut it. 2nd, we bound it. 3rd, we threshed it.

Here's the way the mind works. In the 19th century when we mechanized the harvest, we built 3 machines: a cutter, a binder, and a thresher.

Here's the way the mind works. Time passes. Wait 1 second, we don't have to harvest grain in 3 steps with 3 machines. We can COMBINE them.

Here's the way the mind works. There once were machines, analog machines, named a telephone, a fax, a camera, a record player, a typewriter.

Here's the way the mind works. When the machines were digitalized they made individual machines: a telephone, a fax, a camera, a typewriter.

Here's the way the mind works. Time passes. Wait 1 second, we don't need all of these. We can COMBINE them. And there it is in your hands.

Every day, I arrive early, wait by the door, greet my students as they enter. "Welcome! I'm Michael Martone. I'll be your instructor today."

Waiting in the doorway for the students to arrive, I borrowed this from Montessori. "Hello, I'm Michael Martone, your instructor for today."

When a student arrives, I not only greet them and introduce myself (every day is a new day!) but also ask, "What would you like to do today?"

Standing in the hallway, I wait for my students. I share the space with other students (on benches, on the floors). They mine their devices.

The waiting students "mine" their devices. I dig the pun. "Hey!" I say to the closest one, her thumbs digging in, "Are you writing a poem?"

It's unfair to think, I think, that the devices have transformed their users into mindless zombies. It is quiet. But mining is not mindless.

The hallway is dim, deep. Light, generated by the devices, bounces off the blank faces. No, not blank, concentrated faces, pools reflecting.

No, not zombies, more like ghosts. The hallway is haunted. The students, waiting for their classes to begin, are here but they are not here.

I haunt this haunted hallway. I am alone, deviceless, my hands not folded in this new gesture of prayer. Hey, I say, are you writing a poem?

"A poem?" She's alive! Not a Texting Dead. Called back from elsewhere. Here, now, she thinks "poem," thinks what kind of text she's texted.

This is just to say . . . Poems are their frames, the occasions of their writing and reading. The polycarbonate windowpane. The refrigerator door.

It all started at Penn State, Altoona. I gave a reading there. Many confused freshmen had been forced to attend. Not the best idea. I began.

Altoona, before smartphones. I look up as I read. They don't think I can see them. They're freshmen, hunched over. "Are you texting?" "Yes!"

You're texting? Yes, they shout. They're freshmen. I've stopped reading. Who are you texting? They point to each other in the room. So cute.

"Hey," I say, "I want in on this." I'm reminded that we're living now in a vast electromagnetic soup, swimming with schools of digital text.

I give them my cell number. Text me, I tell them as I start to read my own texts. Text me. How am I doing? Or text each other. The number is

They do text me as I read. My clamshell phone, turned off in my pocket. Someone loves my bow tie, I learned later. Another thinks I'm funny.

That night in Altoona after the reading, I graze the text messages, electronic marginalia. It's reader response critique, impulse and pulse.

The phone's transformed. Distraction to attraction. It is a record of attentive back-channeling. They listened with their prehensile thumbs.

Every public reading after, I hope the host commands, at the intro's end, to turn off your phones so I can say, as I start, to turn them on.

Now, as I give out my number, I beg their pardon. I'll answer but later, after. I am not like you kids, I say, who can answer while reading.

I try to respond to the cache of texts waiting for me after I read. I have a keyboard keyed to numbers. These are essays on the tiny screen.

Close, close readings. I squint at the worried responses, sometimes retrieved in three or four bursts. The questions I'm at pains to answer.

In the end, I do answer them, the texts swept up through the evening of reading. At times, the conversation continues. My number remembered.

I give a reading. I give out my number. That number lodged in the phone's memory. That story I read that night lodged in that user's brain.

My son knows my number is out there. At the AWP, he tweets followers that my number lurks on their phones, suggests they "drunk dial Dad."

At the convention, the texts home. Fragments of fragments the writers retain, what has stuck from a reading long gone, from who knows where.

They're anonymous, these texts from the past. My phone is ancient, no way to ID. The text and the texter present with brief sweet intimacy.

I carry on conversations still, folded in my phone in my pocket, commenced, a pulsar blurted at an event, braided with words I floated then.

In class, the phones are always "on." They have my number. Like freshman in Altoona, they think I cannot see them. They can't not not stop.

Komboloi, Greek "worry" beads. Transitional object. Comfort object. That string of beads manipulated. Fiddled with. Thumbed. Toyed. Worried.

I watch them address the screens of their phones, write, and I'm reminded of komboloi, those beads. I like their worry of words, of letters.

They are on a loop, the beads of the komboloi. The words on the cellphones too. Logostatic, feeding back. Cybernetic. A worry and a comfort.

Donald Barthelme: "The principle of collage is one of the central principles of art in this century." My class is collaged, one big collage.

Colleagues eye collages warily, suggest that student writers will find such formal compositions too difficult & frustrating & foreign & and.

"Really?" I say to those who think collage is too "experimental" or too "advanced" for "beginning" writers. "Have you seen how they see TV?"

Right now, writing this, I have a dozen tabs open in my browser. One is for a Wikipedia entry on komboloi, another on Barthelme and collage.

Collage. My writing exercises are varieties of collage. A commonplace book. A taxonomy (fictional or not). Exercises in style after Queneau.

Collage is about accumulation, a coral reefing of words, sentences, paragraphs. A little writing each day, a week. Don't try to connect them

now, I tell them. What do you want to worry? We worry about association, about juxtaposition, the synaptic leap that white space represents.

One student loved guns, wrote one piece a week. His first firearm described. A fiction of another. Hunting with his father. Technical specs.

All of these individual subjects blogged, feeding an electronic feed, even collected into an analog handmade book, bullets and billet-doux.

We consider cuts. The Great Train Robbery. The first time in film. A cut to simultaneous action. How that cut. Could not be. Processed. Cut.

The mind and combines again. Film. Time. It took time to see that a film was not simply a recorded play, time to see this new way of seeing.

Now, you, my students, I process hundreds of cuts easily in our reading, our writing. We're more arrangers than writers. We stutter and cut.

The material nature of texts. How is it physical? Collage insists we handle that text. Collage resists writing that insists on transparency.

The new instruments of writing are so handy. They're so handheld. These new devices have, perhaps, defamiliarized the hand, the handmade.

I go beyond. The postcard, analog Tweet. I hand out cards to the class. Postcards don't need to be defamiliarized. They're not even familiar.

The postcard. They hold them in their hands. A remarkable piece of technology, I say. The picture side pictures the campus we walk each day.

You use this piece of paper, address it, attach to it this special, smaller, adhesive-backed piece of paper purchased in an official office.

We'll then search the city for specially constructed blue metal boxes equipped with a clever slot into which we'll place the prepared cards.

From the blue box, the stamped postcard will be hand-delivered to the addressee, carried by an uniformed officer of the Federal government.

There's nervous twitter. They're vaguely familiar with the post office and the mail, but such an alien description warps them even further.

Those students who have written postcards have written postcards on vacation. I suggest we write about this campus as if we are on vacation.

Can they get their minds around it? See the campus in this other way and write about it as if it's all new. They'll send them to themselves.

They never get mail. And now the mail they will get will be from this strange place that actually occupies the same space as this here here.

There are all the different precincts on postcards. The address field. The stamp square. The postal barcode box. The message leftover blank.

I like it when a postcard's picture has been written on. Here, a resort hotel's balconied facade. An ink sketched speech bubble (I am here).

We are walking the campus, crossing at a crosswalk when we notice the acid-yellow diamond-shaped warning sign, its matte shadow man walking.

The yellow sign is now framed by strobing LEDs, a book-sized solar panel powers it. It attracts our attention to how attention is attracted.

Even after all the LEDs, the neon yelling yellow, the sign, invisible, the crosswalk too. It must evolve with our accumulating indifference.

We stare at the warning sign warning. What else to add to the matte man? A Hula-Hoop? Wheels on his stumps? A halo? Anything to hook an eye.

Buried behind buildings (the theater, the power plant) the spring bubbles. It has been here forever. It's why the university was built here.

The students never knew, overlooked it on the way to classes. A muddy sump maybe. The coal bunker leached sulfur up above. Black backwater.

It is something to see, to take the moment to see. It is like a secret passage that appears after a spell. It seeps more detail as we stare.

The Russians say it is our task to make the stone stony again. And we are. We do. The generic shadow on the shingle and schist washes away.

Across the street, there's another kind of not seeing. A motor pool deemed ugly by the school draped in screened fences and overgrown hedge.

That camouflage means to double down, make our nonchalant not-seeing blinder. But it only makes me want to see what I'm not supposed to see.

Hidden behind the fences and hedges with the tractors and fuel drums, we see the parabolic arch of a Quonset hut sided with corrugated rust.

Quonset, I tell them, is one of my favorite words. I ask after theirs. Named, "Quonset" can be seen. We wonder why this or that word sticks.

This building has bona fides. This particular hut is historic. It's the last of a slew thrown up postwar to house the returning GI Billers.

The campus is filled with faux classical temples capped with every order of capital, cupola, and metope. But here this modest culvert means.

There's an old pond nearby. I have the students search for Basho's haiku old pond / frog jump into / watersound floats up on their screens.

They're shy. Why is this one of the most famous poems in the world? We talk about the sudden turn. The way sight is swallowed up by a sound.

The pond once was the college pool. A hidden pump agitates the surface in ripples. A frog does jump, disrupting the disruption's disruption.

The university advertises itself: Alabama touching lives. The visual? A student's face lights up, enlightenment radiates outward into space.

Watching the pond's ripples dissipate, I ask the writers to imagine someone somewhere, bored, distracted. Now, now text something, nothing.

"Make nothing happen." It's a double take the writer takes. The ply, play. The slipperiness of language, its amphibian nature. Its bothness.

In short, text, but text differently. Think of it as a gift. A sudden emergence in that someone's phone, a startled passenger on a lily pad.

Leap a leap, I say to them, and they heave to. They are coiled on the bank like students about to strike. Their thumbs skate like water bugs.

I ask them to turn the volume up. I want to hear the whoosh the machine makes as the message goes. We've talked about Hermes. Here's Hermes.

They consider such compositions "random." This is all very random. Yes, exactly. We're looking for the meaningful composition of the random.

There's a murmuration of whooshes as their texts launch. The texts infiltrate the electromagnet porridge, a kind of slurp, a splash, a hush.

And now they read their work, but tell me where the message went. "To my brother in Oregon." "Oregon!" I shout, reminding them to be amazed.

No matter where they send, I am amazed. I am amazed. I tell that that, I am. You wrote something like that, and there it is there like that.

They read the missives. Their recipients. Think of the someone, somewhere, whose phone alerts just now, like that, unwraps a knotted nothing.

One last thing I ask once they've shared their texts. I ask that they turn their phones to vibrate, set at eleven, while we contemplate the pond.

Scattered, yes, randomly by the pond. One or two or more phones strike up a ribbit. Ribbit. Ribbit. The phones transmit a workshop of frogs.

WW/MM

MM: I have always taken exception to the label of "experimental" applied to writing. It just does not work as a descriptor for me because it depends on a foil like "traditional" or, even worse, "normal" as its contrast, its other. So, I was very pleased to read the detailed generic work you perform in the "Author's Note" that opens your book, the finely and suggestively (for me after the scree of mine above) titled *Multiply Divide*. The "Author's Note" maps out three major forms for the pieces that follow, along with the permutation of the various characteristics into even more elaborate or spliced formal structures.

Right? Don't call me (or you, perhaps?) an "experimental" writer. I like to think of myself as a "formalist," adept (I hope) at identifying and deploying the many structures, styles, and strategies of language while also manipulating the frames in which the forms appear.

I appreciate how you tread that minefield of binaries, especially the fiction/ nonfiction one as well as the nonfiction/truth category. It always strikes me that prose writers do worry those backward-slashed boundaries while poets breeze right through the porousness (as you characterize it) or ignore them altogether. No one ever, it seems, talks of a "nonfiction" or "fiction" poem. No, the more interesting divide for me (and you put it into play right away) is the one between the lyrical and the narrative. The "Author's Note" prepares me for this. I have been alerted to the fact (Ha! Fact!) that the following work will resist the existential nature of writing itself. Writing is a sequential medium. It lines up. It has, by nature, a beginning, middle, and end. But I am ready for the lyric. And I am prepared for this cussedness, this desire to resist the linear nature of language. And with that I will "cut" to you.

WW: I wrote the Author's Note to maintain the spirit of accuracy I hoped to deliver elsewhere in the book, but I suppose it does complicate some people's understanding of genre. The places I write about in *Multiply/Divide* are, for the most part, real. Because of this, there's a lot more I can do formally. But when one writes about a world that is wholly imagined, a speculative space, how do you ensure unity between the pieces and approaches? An anthology of characters written by multiple authors creates a set of challenges related to scope, continuity, and structure. I am interested in how you resolved these complications and managed to evoke a place that feels real.

I did note that *Winesburg, Indiana* moves as a progression of characters, which seems to follow in the tradition of speculative regional anthologies like: Edgar Lee Master's *Spoon River Anthology* (1915), Jean Toomer's *Cane* (1923), and of course, Sherwood Anderson's *Winesburg, Ohio* (1919). All of these were published early in the twentieth century and in some ways offered observation and acknowledgment of the kind characters also embraced by the Victorian novel, the underclasses and downtrodden. The politics behind this kind of writing would evolve into a social realism, a driving impulse in the most memorable of the late-century novels.

But we stand at a very different moment in history. Notable differences between now and then include the casual acceptance of perpetual war; the decline of the nation as a principal economic entity; the dissolution of local economies; and the dismantling of public institutions, including schools, libraries, and universities. These conflicts, while in the background, are still felt. I was especially interested in the portrayal of the university, as one figures prominently in the lives of several characters in *Winesburg, Indiana*. From the professors to those who clean up their offices and those who were drawn to town because of it, the university casts a shadowy image of distant opportunity. In this, I can't help but to think of Thomas Hardy's grim meditation on a similar proximity in *Jude the Obscure* (1895).

MM: It surprised me that you focused on the social realism of *Winesburg, Indiana*'s progenitors as the harmonic. Of course it is difficult reflecting upon this book, even as I wrote a chunk of it and devised the conception of the fictional town, as so much of it was out of my control, written by a cadre of other writers only deflected by a few restrictions as to place details. But I do think of the book as very "social" and in fact, more and more, think of publishing as more like political organizing than the gatekeeping of taste and promoting something as "good" or "bad."

And it was very interesting to me when "the university" showed up in what the contributors contributed. For my part, I was less interested in the politics, the social commentary, or even the muckraking nature of the early Twentieth Century realists and naturalists. What interested me was the construction, in a book like *Winesburg, Ohio*, of the modern character that now, through Freud's invention of "depth," has become reality. I tell you sometime I think Freud was the greatest fiction writer of them all. He instills in me a kind of professional envy. Oh, to have created the "id" or the "subconscious" or any of the complexes and dynamics of the secret life and buried childhood traumas. Politically, I think *Winesburg, Ohio* is the gateway drug to the emerging literate middle class and "the tragedy of the broken teacup," as Frank Norris characterized American Domestic Realism. The acceptance of these deep character tropes focuses the struggle internally and personally and not outwardly, politically, or socially.

There is, for me, a pun in the name of this town of inwardly looking people. We played with calling the book and the town *Whinesburg, Indiana,* the municipality at the end of the psychoanalytic era, now, perhaps, all talking but very little cure.

And this brings me back to that other binary of yours I was thinking about, the lyric/narrative. Freud is all about story, about shaping the stuff that happens into stuff that means to mean. There are consequences. There are insights and, yes, even lessons to be gleaned. Perhaps Jung is more lyrical? For me he is more associative and social. I admired "Chicago Radio," "In Search of a Face," and "Post-logical Notes on Self-Election" for the full-blown collaged and, dare I say, lyrical explosions they are. Almost all of the other pieces in the book use the white space, that synaptic leap of the lyric, to invite the reader into the piece, to make meaning collaboratively. Just your use of litany is stunning. A list of city names (Whinesburg/Winesburg—Ha!) is so evocative to me. These pieces of prose might tell a "story," but the stories they tell all have such frayed and "unfinished" seams. They are not a line so much as a complicated blot that keeps spreading, enveloping.

I like to think that *Winesburg, Indiana*, in the sense that a story means to make sense, has stopped making sense.

Does that make sense to you?

ww: Yes. It does.

The seams between the stories in *Winesburg, Indiana* feel like massive caverns of implication, and that distance is imaginatively productive. I feel a sense of mystery about this place, and I also remain aware of the possibility that it may be a metaphor or set piece for some other kind of symbolic reckoning.

One story I keep coming back to is "Walt 'Helper' Voltz." His diction offers a remarkable contrast to his insistence on the importance of routine in his profession, what he describes over and over as "just moving the trains back and forth." Early on in his account, he sings "Dah, dah, dit, dah dah dah." I kept coming back to this character for his humor and perspective. Right there in the middle of the book, he suggests that besides moving the train back and forth across the short distance of track, there is no long-term solution for inertia, for succumbing to stasis, for turning to rust.

After making this plain, he asks, "Is that enough human interest, this old man and his little train?" as if he knows he's illustrating something else untold. He looks around, then describes the foliage, one I also recognize from growing up in Michigan: "the ditch-weed, the paw-paw, the sassafras saplings" appearing as urgency—the verdure's ambition to forever obscure all traces of industry in the landscape. Steel and iron fail to thrive like native species.

In Helper's story there is also nostalgia for the active rail yard, the good old days when shipments were coming in and out of Winesburg. His whining (or pining) for movement, speed, and the mystery of boxcars that come from someplace else is so moving, it is evidence that Winesburg remains small, that it has not yet succumbed to sprawl. That fact operates like a lamppost in the middle of the book, one that illuminates all the opportunities that never came to a place such as this. Still, the nostalgia for the time that did not deliver prosperity lingers without irony. I get it but also feel this way of thinking makes no sense. Is it a yearning that seems especially American? It feels that way.

Dah, dah, dit, dah dah dah.

MM: I have just returned from a birthday trip where the present was a cab ride in a locomotive on the Great Smoky Mountains Railroad. I am a sucker for railroads—I like to see it lap the miles—and am a lifelong subscriber to *TRAINS: The Magazine of Railroading*. So, at sixty, I had my first chance to ride along in the cab. In this engine, the "deadman" mentioned by Walt had been disabled—we weren't really going that far or fast. But in the story, I think, I was interested in that toggle switch between life/death as well as (and you pressed all the right buttons) the one switching back and forth through time—past/present. I think of writing (I think) and its linear nature, like a rail line, and I do think of that "deadman" switch not as an accelerator, of course, but as a manifestation of mindfulness. It must be depressed, punched constantly, or the train will think the controller is no longer present and shut down, go into emergency braking. Yes, the linear nature of the tracks and the cyclical nature of the repetitive gesture of the engineer in the cab is a dance of the lyric and narrative again for me. Like reading, writing is the illustration of going, but it is, as you point out, also about going back and forth in one place.

I like trains, too, because they are so much about geography, place. The names of lines—Chicago & Northwestern; Gulf, Mobile & Ohio; Louisville & Nashville; Baltimore & Ohio; Pennsylvania; and the Cleveland, Cincinnati, Chicago and St. Louis (the Big Four)—remind us that a solid real ribbon of rail physically connects one place to another. What caught my eye above was the mention of your growing up in Michigan. And that got me thinking about "place" in both our books and in our writing. *Multiply/Divide* is so very much about identity, and it weaves masterfully all of the category strands that make up who we are and who we say we are—race, class, gender—including one—place—that I think usually goes so discounted.

I think I do, often (weirdly?), identify as a "Hoosier" first, but what does that even mean? Does "growing up in Michigan" or wherever make us us more or less than any other lens we employ to see who we are? I do think it is interesting that actual political power is still invested in place. We vote in wards and precincts, townships and counties, cities and states. Your book worries place. There are, here, a lot of places to worry. The two Manhattanville pieces meditate on race, class, and gender and use a place as a foil to throw those categories into high relief. The physical aspects of place deflect the humans living within the boundaries of place at the same time the place itself is transformed by the inhabitants of place. Much of what you write about is the power of all these categories to define even while they are apparently invisible to us. They are both multipliers and divisors of who we are. Your work, then, is the work of defamiliarization. Also, you make clear in that making clear, "time" is a crucial component of place. You conclude "Manhattanville, Part Two" with this:

> Opinions of the future of the neighborhood remain divided, as it is still a place where one may walk without recognition of change or history.

I think *Multiply/Divide* does do the work of "making the stone stony again." We "recognize," rethink, categories of identity we have glossed as well as sense the physical nature of time and place.

ww: I'm thinking about my lens in terms of Winesburg, specifically as I read it with regards to considering race. I notice that most of the characters don't seem to think about race defining the place where they are, though there is that moment when Deanne Stovers tells us, "Mama says I could pass for a used cotton ball." "White" in that piece stands in for the wedding dress, for virginity, and the unsullied soul—which in her case is a kind of put-on or performance that torments her. Characters can be very aware of how they look: Professor Helen C. Andersen fears her large forehead makes her look like a man, and Clyde suffers from a size-nineteen left foot, but overall there is little attention to what whiteness means in this space or how whiteness normalizes each of their oddities.

Perhaps my "growing up in Michigan" informs this sensitivity. I can't imagine not worrying about place. As I child I witnessed firsthand the effects of a collapsing auto industry. Racial segregation followed economic discord. I can't imagine industrial spaces without thinking about how egalitarian industry towns could be when everyone was making money (if you were a man, of course), but how quickly paranoia, xenophobia, and fear of change return when economic opportunity dwindles. So for me, Winesburg is also a place worthy of worry and reconsideration.

In towns that were unable to grow and prosper after the 1970s, there is great nostalgia for the period of industrial expansion. Even after factories and plants close, looking back allows those empty buildings to remain fixtures in the contemporary landscape. The period of expansion was a brief moment in American history, but it's a powerful narrative trope that key works like *Winesburg, Indiana*, have been taking on for nearly a hundred years. That past can't be imagined with a more racially diverse cast of characters because each will bring their own origin myth to the history and complicate it with conflicts that contradict the narrative of "blending in" in different ways.

MM: I live in Alabama now, though when I write I still write about Indiana and the Midwest. I have found that when I tell people from Indiana that I write about Indiana, they always ask, "Why?" But when one of my student writers here mentions that he or she would like to write about Alabama or the South, everyone chimes in, "What kept you?" I have always found it interesting that some places, subjects, and people seem "storied," while at the same time other places, subjects, and people do not. But I have had to make do. And I find I have been interested in the flatness, the emptiness, and the ruin and waste that is now the place of place in Indiana and the Midwest.

You're right, of course, about that other absence in the book, the absence of color. And color itself gets absorbed, for me, into the optics of invisibility. I think the Midwest generally and Indiana more specifically is culturally transparent, hidden in plain sight. The flyover indeed.

Invisibility. I am reminded of another seemingly unseen event happening right now connecting me here in the place I live to there, the place I write about. When my mother and dad were alive they would drive down from Indiana for a visit, parking their car in the driveway out in front of the house. I live in West End near Stillman College, demarcated by Martin Luther King Jr. Boulevard. The neighborhoods in West End have in the past been somewhat diverse, but now they are predominately black. Early in our time here, with my parents' visiting, there was a knock at my door, and an African American neighbor asked me, "Who's from Fort Wayne?" He had read the county code on the license plate of my parent's car, "2," and knew it was Allen County. With that introduction we exchanged the stories of our migrations. And here the invisibility part is made visible: He and his family had participated in the Great Migration up from Alabama, largely unseen and mostly unreported, during the 1940s and 1950s and settled in Fort Wayne, where, it turned out, my mother had taught members of his family English at Central High School. Now, he and his family had returned home. I "saw" all around me this migration of people disparately and desperately moving through, around, between place and places, largely in small ways that are multiplied in aggregate without anyone in the position of noticing.

For me, that has always been the main drama of America: mobility versus stability. And in all that drama, mobility wins out. Capital is fluid. Labor is not. The great irony of Detroit is that it was the place that created (at the expense of the stability of other places) the means of movement that ended up destroying it. Henry Ford's Greenfield Village, like Winesburg, I think, reeks with nostalgia. Ford, who proudly provided a cheap means to move, re-created in the factory's backyard the pristine and "stable" nineteenth-century village of his youth. Cars are banned (save a few Model T's—benign snakes in the garden). Greenfield Village is what we call with a straight face "living history." Meanwhile, the physics of dying history is happening right outside the gates. Grass is growing in the streets of Detroit (streets that made it so easy to move), a city constructed for millions now home for a few hundred thousand.

Your book ends with two meditations of migration, "When the Sea Comes for Us" and "Norway." In the first, you ask the reader to think about the land and the sea, the usual signs of stability, cast now in the role of the migrant. And in the latter, you depict the rare event, for America, of an externally directed immigration. America's migrations are mostly internal, the notable exceptions being Liberia and the defeated Confederate move to Latin America. We people stay put but are constantly agitated internally. Restless. Restless.

Even here, at the end of the book. And at the end of this exchange. We send these populations of words back and forth, hither and yon, through the electromagnetic soup now teeming with, yes, restless restless texts. Each of my iterations was written in different places on different machines. We would like to think the books we have been thinking about are stable platforms, but we know that they are built on sand. Literally, sand. Chips off the silicon chip block.

A "fact" is a thing done, and once it is done it is gone. Left behind is the residue of the happening, residue that we have been sifting through both here and in the books we have made. Collage, juxtaposition, association, arrangement. That is my takeaway. Lyrical nonfiction is prose that rhymes, not sonically, but via the glancing and glossing of thought. The ability to make something visible through reflection.

ww: It's interesting to me that you bring up Detroit. My father worked for General Motors. In fact, most of my family in the area worked in an automobile plant or for the UAW. Heck, I was born in Flint, and I worked there at the Fisher BOC One plant as a university student. I have seen the challenges an industry in decline can bring. Though the region struggled to get on sound economic footing throughout most of my life there, I am not nostalgic for personal upheavals of the Rust Belt. Many did not survive.

I also think the kind of invisibility you describe, at least in Detroit, was a response to the city becoming a black majority due to "white flight" after the city burned following civil unrest in 1967.

This is not the only story of Midwestern invisibility through destabilization. It happened in Ohio with the auto, rubber, glass, and ceramics industries, too.

These are facts. But sometimes fiction tells the story better.

Maybe because I came of age in the Midwest during a period of rapid and significant economic decline, I have always been interested in writing about the shifting sand under my feet, the undertow, wherever I find myself at home. Race functions as that undermining element when other people's perceptions of me have greater value than my own. This is also true with work, or more accurately, the lack of it.

Toward the end of your book, we encounter Inspector 4, whose job is to be in control of the eraser. And indeed, as the piece moves on, there is erasure. More of the inspector's content disappears, including letters in the words. The inspector attempts to repeat what has been said before, but so many letters are missing that it is difficult to discern meaning. Erasure is an apt metaphor for the experiences of feeling invisible or destabilized. There is much common experience in that still to mine.

I enjoy how it engages with the conventions of form, yoking it, then letting it loose.

In closing, I'll argue that the last two pieces of my book, rather than being meditations on migration, are more about what it means to never really have a home or a homeland. But while that lack of geographical inheritance might seem tragic to some, there is freedom in knowing that you can survive despite that rootlessness. More important than surviving is the power in knowing you can change, that you can adapt to whatever world in which you put yourself.

Footnotes[i] & Endnotes[ii]

It seems clear now that my relationship with David took place in the margins. There was a stretch of brief proximity as we lived in the same town for a while.[1] We both wrote prose, but each wrote a very different kind of prose. We both hailed from the Midwest, growing up there in overlapping sequence. I was older. Being writers and teachers, we shared the Venn diagrammatical sandwich of writers, teachers, and students we knew in common, those elliptical lozenges of coincidence. David had written a story about a story my teacher[iii] had written, that kind of happenstance intersection. There were, when we were proximate, a few gifts exchanged—books, our own and others, tokens. On my desk now there is the small wreck of residue of our relationship—some letters[2] and postcards, several books grappling us together through citation or acknowledgement. In an essay, David mentions some writing of mine. In a copyright notice, he acknowledges the first appearance of one of his essays in a book I had edited.[3] Tedious. Tenuous. Tiny. Our connections were a kind of sustained static—subliminal, subsonic, subordinate.[4] It was, at best, casual, this relationship, informal, trivial even. But trivial in ways trivial—both as a nexus of unimportant minutia, its accumulated uselessness, but also trivial, literally, in that we met (when we actually met) at a kind of crossroads, a crossroads rank with the other kind of detail, insignificant, no doubt, but a crossroads nevertheless. Our lives as roads crossing, a crossroads of such insignificant crossroads, the intersection of the crucial crux of the askance, the glancing blow that landed full force at the bottom of the page. We were, to each other, each other's footnotes. David, who in his work reinvigorated this limbic device, moved it beyond the parasitic, made it, once again, symbiotic to the body copy, made it, at last, the body's copy. This, then, is the place to remember him, this crossroad where David annotated his soul to the devil. To be a footnote in his narrative! To have him as a footnote in mine! Our little lives, petty and puny, rendered important, if at all, in afterthought, digression, totally random dude-ness, a Bernoullic tactic of tacking, that tracks as mere tendency and tender tending. But it is clear now that's where he lived, in the ever-expanding running sole at the bottom of the page, the infinite open-endedlessness, the possibility inherent in that begging space down in the heels on bended knee, there to be filled with everything and more, one foot in the door of the Library of Babel and the other foot always always in the grave, the rest of the rest.[iv]

1. I took no note of the first time I met David Foster Wallace in person. It was in Syracuse,[v] New York, where I taught for five years at the university there. I was working on a book called *Pensées: The Thoughts of Dan Quayle*, a thin volume by design, twelve thoughts in the voice of the then newly former vice president and David was working on *Infinite Jest*, that gigantic digression within digressions. We didn't talk about any of that, I know. I believe Linda Perla, a student of mine who had met David at a meeting, introduced us. Once, I gave him a ride home from campus.[1] It was snowing. It always seemed to snow in Syracuse.[vi] It seems to have always been snowing in Syracuse.[vii] David lived then in a few rooms in a house with a rotting porch across the street from the food co-op. I remember little of what we talked about that time except for the anecdote about the buckwheat flour, locally milled, available in the neighboring store. I told him I had, until recently, been able to use the buckwheat hulls, a waste product the mill was happy for me to haul, as mulch in my garden. The downy, soft-gray hulls looked like sooty urban snowdrifts drifting up against the rugosa roses in the few months it didn't actually snow.[2] I had just been informed, I told him, that there was no more mulch to be had at the mill.

177

FOOTNOTES & ENDNOTES

1. It might have been after a lunch at the faculty club. If it was that time, it was when I had introduced him to Lewis Hyde's book *The Gift: Imagination and the Erotic Life of Property*. I always include the book as a reference book in the workshops I teach, as it worries the two economies artists operate within, the gift economy and the commodity one, and the consequences of each on one's art and life. What does it mean to say that one is "gifted" as a writer begins the rumination? I knew Lewis when I lived in Boston. My copy of *The Gift* I found in a used bookstore. Lewis had already signed it and inscribed it to a young seminary student on the occasion of his graduation. Lewis was amused that the gift of *The Gift* had not stuck with the original receiver but was now in my hands. A gift, his book contends, is property that stays in motion, thus its appellation as "erotic." So it was amusing that this gift about gifts had now fallen to me to do its work. And I told David the story of my copy. In the book, Lewis, who had worked as a counselor in rehabilitation, examines recovery programs as gift economies, suggesting that the efficacy in treating the condition depends on the absence of a commodified cure. David was taken by the book, not simply because he, at that moment, was working on *Infinite Jest*, but also because of what the book had to say about competitive markets as opposed to collaborative enterprise and in what way is the artist isolated and part of a larger concern. *The Gift*, my gift, was important to him, I think. Years later, he gave the famous commencement address at Kenyon College, where Lewis taught at the time and still teaches. Lewis wrote me that David had remembered me to him when he was on campus, sitting down to talk about Lewis's book.

2. Worse than the relentless snowfall was the even more relentless cloud cover. Syracuse receives, on average, fewer than sixty days of available sunlight a year. Both the clouds and the snow the clouds produce are a result of the lake effect—colder air moving across the relative warmer water of the great lake. I always admired that notion, the notion of "available" light, light light enough to cast a shadow. I remember us "huddled" in the gloaming going to gloom.

The product was now being shipped to Japan, where the hulls were used to stuff delicate pillows that were then returned here and sold at co-ops, head shops, and health food stores as brand new New Age[3] bedding.

2. In a handwritten footnote in a letter[4] I have from David he writes:[5]

Really? Dr. Frank Burns?

This is a reference to a footnote in my book, *The Blue Guide to Indiana*,[6] an after-thought, really, where I attached a fictional author's note to the end of my fictional travel guide in which I report I was delivered at birth by a Dr. Frank Burns, a fictional character from the television show M*A*S*H, and where the same Dr. Frank Burns attends Michael Martone's mother's death. Later,[7] I would expand this after-thought into a whole book of such contributor's notes, many of which[8] were about the death of Michael Martone's mother.[9] The "D" of the handwritten "Dr." in David's

3. I received a letter from David soon after he was hired to teach in California confessing to some disquiet with the move and with teaching. "As I get more and more uneasy with the psychodynamics of the standard workshop—and in contemplation of having to start teaching very very bright kids at Pomona next fall . . ." There is a palpable difference between the students of the Midwest and the ones on each coast. Not so much in the brightness factor but in the ratio of sound to silence generated. I imagine there was a lot of silence to fill in Normal. And didn't I see, in one of the last of David's contributor's notes, David cracking wise on how it seemed everyone now lived in California. My last contact with David was a message brought back to Alabama by a colleague who had given a lecture at Pomona (she is in Renaissance studies), and David had said to say "Hey." As I type this, I have begun to worry that I really do not have the rights or the right to quote from the letters, that the letters David wrote to me even as they are in my possession are not mine to use without permission. I think that is right. A case won in court by Salinger perhaps. But then again, who will read this far or this deep? I couldn't really help David as he transitioned from snowy Syracuse to normal Normal to sunny California. I do feel bad about that. I put off writing back, perhaps, still flummoxed by my own move to Alabama, below the bug line, the line below which, because it never gets cold enough, insects do not die over the winter.

4. Dated: 10-7-01 in the style of a memo, headed in all caps, a kind of re: "BOMBING ONGOING—CAN'T SEE WHAT ELSE TO DO BUT GO ON WITH TODAY'S LIST OF STUFF WHILE SORT OF INAUDIBLY WHIMPERING . . ."
    From: David Wallace, RR2 Box 361, Bloomington, 61704 IL
    To: Michael Martone, PO Box 21179, Tuscaloosa, AL 35402

5. In blue ink.

6. The occasion of the letter above was, among other things, to thank me for sending him a copy of the book—"I have four mss.'s I've promised to read for people before Thanksgiving, so my fun reading will be on hold for about six weeks—*BGI* and Curt White's *Requiem* will be the first two Fun Things I do—the *Blue Guide* first because a quick look at the INNOCULATION section ensures me it will be more fun."

7. Four years later.

8. As this one was.

9. My own mother, who is still alive at this writing, was always uneasy that her son would write and publish so many occasions of her dying, documented in realistic fashion, by her real son, Michael Martone, who shared the name with the character in the book *Michael Martone*. I believe I just have trouble ending things, have trouble with the world's insistence that things end, that stories end, that everything ends, and that here, in this genre of the contributor's note, an endnote after all, there could be a strategy of resistance to the reality, both aesthetic and organic, that things end. As I liked to point out to my mother, it was true that Michael Martone's mother dies, but in the next note she returns as if nothing had ever happened or that anything ever could happen again.

footnote looks more like the symbol for pi,[10] as does the "D" in the inscribed "David W" of the signature.[11] Pi is perhaps the most well-known irrational number,[12] the endlessly endless fraction that does not repeat or terminate.[13] The vertically angled lines of the Pi-like "D" appear to be parallel, no tie-like stroke tying them together, but out there somewhere, at some vanishing point somewhere off the page, a projection, a trick of our own non-Euclidian perception's perspective, they will meet, a bounded, rounded "D" after all, a kind of pregnancy, an abbreviation as well, "D." An abbreviation, you know what for.

3. I am trying to reconstruct time here. Though I met David in person first in Syracuse, New York, sometime in the early nineties, I had worked with him a few years earlier when I asked him to contribute to a book of essays called *Townships*.[14] For that project, I asked a passel of Midwestern writers to write about the Midwestern townships[15] in which they grew up. David wrote back with "Derivative Sport in Tornado[viii] Alley," a piece about the plain plain geometry of his Midwestern place near Normal, Ill.,[16] the undeniable vectors in the game of tennis, and the stunning high-pressure play of the high-pressure physics of precipitous isobars. The piece ends memorably with David, in the midst of a fierce game of tennis on a blasted rural court in the middle of nowhere, being hurled by a sudden tornado into the cyclone fence of the backstop, the waffle of its mesh imprinting the map of the

10. Π

11. The letter begins in the style of a memo but ends in the style of a letter: "Yrs.," he closes, and then the signature with its pi-like "D," underscored by a typed "Dave Wallace."

12. "e" and √2 are perhaps as equally well known.

13. At the time the letter was written, he must have been working on his book *Everything and More: A Compact History of ¥* for Norton's Atlas Books series Great Discoveries, published in 2003. I did not know that, as I did not know the book even existed until I saw it listed, remaindered, in a Deadalus catalogue after his death.

14. The University of Iowa Press, 1992.

15. The entire country, except for the original thirteen states, have been surveyed with the township grid, the six-mile by six-mile square subdivided into thirty-six one-square-mile sections. My thesis was that only in the Midwest did the grid of the township take hold as a telling geographic feature, this inscription of the checkerboard of the patchwork quilt, that David picked up on in his contribution, further subdividing the squares within squares down to the boxes within the boxes of the tennis court.

16. Where he would later write to me the letter cited above when he moved to teach at Illinois State University. The last time I saw David Foster Wallace was in Normal, Ill. I had driven there from Chicago. In 1999, I had given a reading in Normal and stopped to have lunch with him there. We talked of insurance, of course (as State Farm is headquartered in adjacent Bloomington), and the strangeness of the actuarial sciences. We ate in an Italian restaurant, though I had suggested the regional hamburger chain Steak n Shake, which had been founded in Normal in 1934 by a man named Gus Belt, who ground the meat for the hamburgers in plain view right behind the counter, generating the restaurant's slogan—"In Sight It Must Be Right." I told David that the heavy china, much of it made by Syracuse China, though most often produced by rival Buffalo, used in the restaurant to this day, adorned with its trademarked winged device reiterating that those things in sight are right, was the china pattern my wife had chosen for the wedding. We had eight settings of the durable platters, plates, saucers, salad and soup and chili bowls, bean pots, and coffee mugs, as well as a dozen glass glasses.

region on his too too solid flesh. Of all the essays in the book (there were twenty-five others) this one certainly made concrete and took seriously the conceit of the township grid, inscribing it in the inscription itself.[17] The essay was literally literal but was it true? Did I ask him that ever? I can't remember that I did, of course, wanting it to be true, as it was too perfect to be true and too perfect not to be.

4. I asked David to contribute a story to a special issue of the *Colorado Review* I was editing. I ended up titling what I thought of—finally—as an anthology more than an edition of a journal *Trying Fiction*. "Attempting," yes, but also "difficult," in what way I wasn't sure. His twenty-five-page fiction, "Another Pioneer," presents as a free-floating footnote, paragraphless, peppered with blank open spaces to be filled in later, and a mean, mean length of utterance, often in the triple digits. He confesses in a letter to me that he wasn't sure, because of its "weirdness"—his word not mine—and density, that he would ever have "found anyplace that'd have taken it." I do like to think that, that the pioneer found the place for this bit of writing,[18] that it will exist here in this quasi anthology. I had to write an introduction to the book and did so in an essay that looks very much like this one—all riddled with footnotes, parentheticals, and asides—but saying, basically, when pieced together, that it is the piecing together that is important, the attempting to make a sense and the repair of conscious mistakes made on the wing, on the fly. Annotation is all. The pulsing blue links embedded now in our hypertexts never seemed the same to me as this kind of enriched, encoded, noted text. In fact, hypertext seems a lame imitation of the act of simply reading. Your eye falls on this word here or a phrase there and your reading mind opens its own second channel, makes its own hyper-leap, always already

17. David's essay is notable in another way as well. The text itself is divided into segmented sections with few paragraphing indentations, and the margins are justified both left and right, so the essay reads, in its gray space, as a series of boxes separated by depthless fields of white space. David included in some of those infinite spaces between the stars a kind of goofy graphic geometry—a blacked-in mostly horizontal rectangle, justified right, a hollow vertical bar centered, an empty square centered, a long flat rectangle outline centered, an empty vertical column hugging the gutter, a black box hard left, the empty empty space at the essay's end. Remember, this was early in the desktop revolution. We were only just then beginning to understand that our Macintoshes were not typewriters. David understood earlier than most, I think, that the drama between the abstract and the concrete (that is writing's bread and butter) had been torqued by this new machine, that a writer now also had at his fingertips this material edge, the bookness of the book, as an aesthetic strategy. Back in Syracuse, we had talked about the critic Hugh Kenner's books *The Counterfeiters* and *The Stoic Comedians*, where he asks why it is the Irish who seem to write the strange, irreal, self-conscious book books. Kenner answers himself by saying that the Irish, having the most developed oral tradition, sensed that when they wrote actual books that this was a whole other matter. A book is not, for the Irish, a transcribed oral tale but a thing unto itself. To demonstrate this Kenner footnotes the sentence[a] and your eyes go to the bottom of the page. And then latter he does it again adding a new footnote superscript to something completely unrelated.[b]

18. It was reprinted in his collection *Oblivion*, published in 2004.

a. See, I made you look to the bottom of the page.

b. See, I made you do it again.

routing rooting around in your own onboard computer. David's texts were all blue already always. Saturated. Maps more detailed than the things they represented. Pioneer indeed.

i. "Footnotes have not had it easy. Their dominance of eighteenth- and nineteenth-century literature and scholarship was both hard won—following many years of struggle—and doomed, as it led to belittlement in the twentieth century. In *The Devil's Details*, Chuck Zerby playfully explores footnotes' long and illustrious history and makes a clarion call to save them from the new world of the Internet and hypertext. In a story that boasts a marvelous plot and a rogues' gallery of players, Zerby examines traditional footnotes and their less-buttoned-down incarnations, as when used by pornographers. Yes, *The Devil's Details* is full of surprises: Zerby hunts down the first bona-fide fully functioning footnote; unearths a multivolume history of Northumberland County, England, that uses one volume for a single footnote; and uncovers a murder plot. He even explains why footnotes are like blind dates." From the promotional copy of *The Devil's Details* by Chuck Zerby.

ii. David Foster Wallace's *Infinite Jest* includes over four hundred endnotes, some over a dozen pages long. Several literary critics suggested that the book be read with two bookmarks. Wallace uses footnotes in much of his other writing as well.*

iii. This was John Barth. We talked about the stories in Barth's *Lost in the Funhouse*, beginning with the beginning interactive story the reader is meant to snip from the page, a long strip printed with the entire story "Once upon a time, there was a story that began" that you were asked to twist and connect the ends, making it into a Mobius solid, an unending surface that would convert the story into an ever-repeating loop. I taught a class at Syracuse that posited the aesthetic tectonic of the American short story had shifted, suddenly, in 1980, from this kind of formal meta-mental falderal to a transparent, realistic narrative. The latter has held sway ever since. David was still smarting from being thought too smart in his own graduate student workshops, a formalist open to the attacks of "too-ness"—too clever, too cold, too self-conscious. It was cold for real in Syracuse, whose oracle, Raymond Carver, had pronounced "No Tricks" in a book called *Fires* he wrote in his house a few blocks away from where we sat.

iv. The letter, dated 10-7-01, was written on Illinois State University stationery. David, a formal stickler I suppose, has, in blue ink, deleted the imprinted address at

* To be a footnote in his narrative! To have him as a footnote in mine! Our little lives, petty and puny, rendered important, if at all, in afterthought, digression, totally random dude-ness, a Bernoullic tactic of tacking that tracks as mere tendency and tender tending. But it is clear now that's where he lived, in the ever-expanding running sole at the bottom of the page, the infinite open-endedlessness, the possibility inherent in that begging space down in the heels on bended knee there to be filled with everything and more, one foot in the door of the Library of Babel and the other foot always always in the grave, the rest of the rest.

the paper's head using the standard copyediting lasso of doom. This was not official business, but personal. A stroke swiftly from the southwest quadrant curving into a loop and then the finishing fillip off into the northeast at a slightly oblique angle. Out goes

COLLEGE OF ARTS AND SCIENCES
Department of English

Then in the center

ILLINOIS STATE
UNIVERSITY

is deleted, the strikeout line springing from the open book of the school's seal below it. Then to the right

Stevenson Hall
Campus Box 4240
Normal, IL 61790–4240
Telephone: (309) 438–3667
Facsimile: (309) 438–5414

Three loose gestural loops. Go. Going. Gone.

v. Syracuse, New York, is where the Brannock Device was invented and is still manufactured there by a family-owned company. The Brannock Device is the instrument used in shoe stores to measure the foot for fit. Machined in steel, its various scales are enameled in different colors: green, purple, red, black. They are sized for men, women, children, athletic shoes, and even ski boots. The thing itself is like a child's busy box. One device handles left and right feet (the heel cup for each foot at each end of the device) and has sliding sleeve for width and an art-deco-inspired knob pointer vectoring to indicate the arch for proper ball-to-heel measurement. Much more sophisticated than the primitive wooden calipers that preceded the device's invention in 1927, a mere pedestrian slide rule. When I left Syracuse a dozen years ago, I called the company to see if I could buy one as a souvenir of my time in the city (I taught at Syracuse University for five years). I talked with a descendant of the inventor who was excited to make the sale. I got a men's. He told me it was an odd business. The device is the Cadillac of such devices. Everyone agrees it is the best manifestation devised by humans for measuring human feet, and due to its near perfection in conception, design, and manufacture, the curve of its obsolescence is almost nil. The moving parts last on this last. It takes a quarter-century for the numbers to finally wear away. Nothing to break. Devices are not pilfered from shoe stores. Expansion in retail shoes proceeds at a petty pace. My transaction was rare—in fact, mine was the first time he could remember anyone buying the device for itself as an object of desire. Odd, when you consider that the widespread fetish for feet and shoes seems not to extend to this diagnostic tool. I display my Brannock device on my office bookshelf. I admire its asymmetrical organic shrapnel curvatures, a kind of no-nonsense abstract sculpture with its own kinetic components I recalibrate when I remember to. The afternoon sun spilling through the window blinds scores the various scales on the device with more gradients of shadow. Mine? 9c.

vi. I don't think we would have had "coffee," as I don't drink coffee. This would have been before the advent of Starbuck's designer beverages. I have no notion if David drank coffee or not. I suppose he did. I do know that I gave him a coffee cup or mug, one of the seconds I collected from the Syracuse China outlet store in Syracuse. Each fall I taught there, I made a pilgrimage out to Court Street on the north side of town to the warehouse-y outlet and worked through the big wooden crates and cardboard bins of rejected restaurant china, heavy durable goods often with the airbrushed detail of pastel-scalloped edging, the rounded lip of the mug already looking kissed, blotted by a Great Depression shade of lipstick. Often the piece would be stamped with decals of diner or yacht club logos, and this would be where the trouble started. Slipped images, double printed, smeared, or out of focus cartoon fixtures. I would gather up a dozen or so each season and give them as housewarming gifts to the new crop of writers in the incoming class at the university. I gave David one of the culls. I would like to think he still had it, had taken the trouble to wrap it up with the Syracuse newspaper, the Normal newspaper, and lugged the mug across country, out to California, where I imagine it is now in some inventory of the estate, some lost coffin in the Spielbergian crane shot of an infinite warehouse of babbling iconic crap. This is what I told the students when I offered them a cup: Here's something from the clay of the place, a proper prop for the writer, profane grail. Bottoms up.

vii. Syracuse's big lake, Onondaga, a vestigial digit in the finger lakes chain, we people on the pavement perversely touted as the most polluted lake in the Western Hemisphere—mercury and soda ash dumped there by Allied-Signal. But I had also heard of vast underwater reefs composed of shards of broken crockery from the factory. Drifts and chains of drifts of smashed and bleaching china encased in ice, one more blasted wasted moonscape.

viii. I am not making this up. I am writing this on January 7, 2009, the first Wednesday of the month, and it is noon and the tornado sirens all began to sound just as I typed the title of David's essay. The sirens are tested the first Wednesday of the month at noon. The sirens rotate, so there is a Doppler effect, that warble wave of ululation.

Acknowledgments

Brooding, the book, took its time to emerge. It is a collection of many occasional essays that found, by the grace and faith of numerous editors and publishers, permanent perches from which to sing. I am eternally grateful and acknowledge their patient and potent collaborations here.

Parts of "Keynotes" appeared in *The Normal School* and *HOW*. The entire piece was part of a collaboration done with Ander Monson as the Keynote Address for the NonfictioNow Conference held in Flagstaff, Arizona, in 2015.

"G♯-Minor Seventh in the Second Inversion," as "Metal Music Machine," first appeared in *Oxford American*.

"Titled: The Title: A Short Short Story's Own Short Short Story" first appeared in *The Rose Metal Press Field Guide to Writing Flash Fiction: Tips from Editors, Teachers, and Writers in the Field*, edited by Tara L. Masih and published by Rose Metal Press in 2009.

"Brooding" first appeared in *Brief Encounters: A collection of Contemporary Nonfiction*, edited by Judith Kitchen and Dinah Lenney and published by W. W. Norton. "Brooding" appeared again in a slightly different form in *Tuscaloosa Writes This*, edited by Brian Oliu and Patti White and published by Slash Pine Press.

"Hermes Goes to College" was first presented at the AWP Conference, then published in *upstreet*. It was later collected by Margot Singer and Nicole Walker in *Bending Genre: Essays on Creative Nonfiction* and published by Bloomsbury.

"Hat Trick" appeared in *Southern Humanities Review*.

"Ostrakons at Amphipolis, Postcards from Chicago: Thucydides and the Invention and Deployment of Lyric History" was first presented at the AWP Conference. *Ascent* published it first, and then it was collected by Margot Singer and Nicole Walker in *Bending Genre: Essays on Creative Nonfiction*, published by Bloomsbury.

"A Bread Crumb Essay: Best American Essays 2005" appeared online as "A Breadcrumb Memoir" at *Essay Daily*.

"Saving the Daylights out of Saving Daylight" was first published in *Indiana Magazine of History*, vol. 102 no. 2 (2006).

"Time in a Vacuum Bottle: A Genealogy" first appeared online at *Hunger Mountain*.

"Thermostat" first appeared in *Nerve*.

"The Zoo We Thought We Bought Bought Us: How the Shape of Shape Shapes Us" was presented at the AWP Conference.

"Some Space" was written for, though not published by, *The New York Times* in the wake of the tornado that struck Tuscaloosa in April 2011. It was first published online by *Brevity* as part of a relief fund effort for the city. I thank the editor, Dinty W. Moore, for coming to the rescue during that desperate time.

"Asymmetry" is reproduced from *Blurring the Boundaries: Explorations to the Fringes of Nonfiction*, edited by B. J. Hollars, by permission of the University of Nebraska Press.

"More or Less: The Camouflage Schemes of the Fictive Essay" first appeared online at *Essay Daily*.

"Dear Miss Hamilton" first appeared as "Letters to Dead Authors: Michael Martone to Edith Hamilton" in *Phd in Creative Writing and Other Stories*.

"I Kill My Grandma Once and for All" was first published by *Oxford American*.

"What Was on My Mind: Face to Facebook with My Mother's Death, July 2012" was published by *Stone Canoe*.

"What Was on My Mind: Face to Facebook with My Father's Death, March/April 2014" first appeared in *Witness* as "Live Blogging My Father's Death."

"Against the Beloved" was published first in *upstreet*.

"Finger Exercises: Tuscaloosa, April 27, 2011" appeared online at *Sweet*.

"Postcards from Below the Bug Line" was originally published in *Ecotone*.

"1-65" first appeared online at *Catching Days*, edited by Cynthia Newberry Martin.

"The Bypass" appeared as a series of articles published in *Fort Wayne Magazine*.

"Old Pond: A Lesson Plan in Tweets" was published in *Getting Personal: Teaching Personal Writing in the Digital Age*, edited by Laura A. Gray-Rosendale for SUNY Press.

"ww/mm" was first published as "Inter-Review: Michael Martone and Wendy S. Walters Talk with Each Other about Their New Books" in *Fourth Genre*, vol. 18 no. 1 (2016), pp. 207–216. I thank Wendy S. Walters for her permission to reprint our "Inter-Review" here once more.

"Footnotes & Endnotes" appeared initially in *Sonora Review* and in the book *Creating Nonfiction*, edited by Jen Hirt and Erin Murphy and published by SUNY Press.

I would like to thank all the Broods I brood with and thank them for their enduring and endearing kindnesses of all kinds. My colony of colleagues below the bug line— Robin Behn, Wendy Rawlings, Joel Brouwer, Kelli Wells, Heidi Lynn Staples, Hali Felt, John Estes, L. Lamar Wilson, William Ulmer, Emily Wittman, Fred Whiting, Deborah Weiss, Albert Pionke, Philip Beidler, Heather White, Yolanda Manora, Patti White—and beyond—Melianie Rae Thon, Sandy Huss, Lex Williford, Joyelle McSweeney, Kate Bernheimer, Peter Streckfus, Bruce Smith, Dave Madden, John Crowley, Charles Baxter, C. J. Hribal, Peter Turchi, Valerie Miner, Rikki Ducornet, Ellen Lesser, Amy Wright, Sejal Shah, Lewis Hyde, Verlyn Klinkenborg, Joseph Geha and Fern Kupfer, Stephen Pett and Clare Cardinal, Sam Pritchard and Tista Horton, Mary Swander, Jane Smiley, Neil Nakadate, Marilyn Sandidge, Kevin Oderman, Rosanne Potter, and Susan Carlson.

Singing each to each, I stay in touch with Jane Dupuis, T. Eric and Ross Brown, Kim Kazemi, Jennie Ver Steeg, Anne Hunsinger, Emily Hopkins, Tobin Anderson, Roberta Bernstein, Jen Reeder and Brian Fryklund, Lisa Howard, Del Lausa, Jenny Colville, Cheryl Dumesnil, Steven Featherstone, Deb Unferth, Vincent Standley, Diana Joseph, Gabe Blackwell, Dan Kaplan, Steve Fellner, David Keith, Erin Stalcup, Lisa Hadley, Cynthia Reeves, Shannon Cain, Robin Black, Samantha Hunt, Ross White, Judy French, Rachel Yoder, Tommy Zurhellen, Dan Waterman, Mindy Wilson, Michael Mejia, Monica Hileman, Zach Vickers, Merritt Tierce, Andy Farkas, Steve Thomas, Farren Stanley, Sara Jane Stoner, Berry Grass, Andy and Sydney Duncan, Jess Richardson, Carl Peterson, Erika Wade, Brian Oliu and Tasha Coryell, Jesse Walters, Alissa Nutting, B. J. Hollars, Jennifer Gravley and Matt Dube, Emma

Furman, Bard Cole, Amalie Flynn, Mark Ehling, Nik De Dominic, Nick Parker, Lauren Choplin, Chinelo Okparanta, E. J. Levy, Harry Thomas, Liz Downs, Natalia Holtzman, Jill Christman and Mark Neely, Chris Chambers, Greg Houser and Betsy Seymour, Colin Rafferty and Elizabeth Wade, Alicia Holmes, Sarah Blackman and John Pursley, Tim Croft, Tessa Fountain, Andy Johnson, Juan Reyes, Laura Didyk, Bret Baker, Annie Hartnett, Jane Sandor, Betsy Hogan, Barrett Hathcock, Michael Lee, Dylan Nice, Matthew Mahaney, Adam Weinstein, Jim Marino, Nicole Rivas, Meg Paonessa, Hugh Sheehy, Collen Hollister and Lucas Southworth, Christhanthi Tsingos, Danilo Thomas and Ashley Gorham, Christopher O. McCarter, Allison Wade, Justin Runge and Kate Lorenz, Brandi Wells, Brian Buckbee, Dara Ewing, and Paul Maliszewski.

Who brooded with me: Peggy Shinner and Sean Lovelace.

I thank the editors who helped with the metamorphosis: Vivian Dorsel, Anna Lena Phillips Bell, Dinty W. Moore, Ander Monson, Patrick Madden, Josh Russell, Robin Hemley, Kelcey Ervick Parker, Barb Shoup, Ned Stuckey-French, Robert Atwan, Miciah Bay Gault, Jen Hirt and Erin Murphy, and Margot Singer and Nicole Walker.

Who serves standing and waiting: Marian Young.

My Pips in Georgia: Bethany Snead, Walter Biggins, Jon Davies, Christina Cotter, David E. Des Jardines, Lisa Bayer.

Thank you to the one who scores the score: Stephen Barnett.

The night I listen to: John Barth, Wendell Berry, Richard Rhodes, Scott Russell Sanders, Mark Kramer.

My harmonic: Susan Neville, Michael Wilkerson, Jay Brandon, Michael Rosen, Ann Jones, Kathy Hall, Nancy Esposito.

Sleep: Christopher Leland and Osvaldo Sabino, Monroe Engel, Russell Pappas, Stella Pappas, Joanne Thomas.

Last notes I hear before sleep each night: Sam and Nick.

First song each morning: Theresa.

Author's Note

Michael Martone was born in Fort Wayne, Indiana. He is the author of several books of fiction and nonfiction, and in the course of publishing and promoting those books, Martone has, upon occasion, given readings of his work at various venues, including colleges and universities, bookstores, churches, and YMCAs. Martone's worst experience as a public reader of his own work happened at a YMCA in Cambridge, Massachusetts. Having given several readings by this point, Martone made sure, in a prereading ritual, that the pages of his manuscript were in order. It always irritates Martone (when he is in the audience for a reading given by other writers) having to witness the seemingly nervous habits of readers shuffling through the pages, searching for the right piece to begin. Admittedly this happens more often with poets, but the practice has spurred Martone to always have his pages in order. So that night right before he began his reading at the Y in Cambridge, Massachusetts, as he forced himself to yawn (an ancient platform speaker's trick to relax the voice), Martone carefully noted the order of his pages by flipping through his manuscript, recounting the numbers in the top right-hand corner. What made the evening such a disaster was that after reading, in order, the first eighteen pages of his story, Martone discovered, as he turned to the final page, that the final page was not there. Looking at the artificial wood-grain of the lectern before him, Martone, chagrinned, announced that he seemed to be missing the final page and then summarized haltingly the missing information to a bemused and embarrassed audience. Since then, Martone always checks to make sure that his pages are not only in order but all there. Over the years, Martone has also had the occasion of organizing and hosting reading series. He has found that, inevitably, the conversation he has before the reading with his visiting readers turns to stories of other reading disasters and mishaps. Martone (while collecting these anecdotes in the hope of one day publishing an anthology of readers' worst readings) noticed that one particular circumstance seemed to befall several poets. It concerned, with slight variations, the visiting poet showing up to read at a college or university to discover his or her host taken ill or taking care of someone who is ill, excusing him or herself before the poet's introduction. The poet then is left in a room alone to discover only a few distracted people in the audience—often one of them is described as a homeless man and the remaining two or three as undergraduate students. The sparsity of the turnout added to the host's departure ratchets up the bleakness of the event. But of course, it gets even worse. The poet introduces him- or herself to the scant audience and reads his or her first poem, and then, in the patter that follows, suggests, as the crowd is so small, that it would be better if they just had an intimate conversation about poetry. The climax is always that one member of the audience asks how long this is going to take since they, the students, are only here to study. The homeless man (if he is in the story) then eats the stale snack crackers and chunks of dried-out cheese from the pitiful reception table. Martone has heard this story delivered by several poets as their worst reading experience. He realizes it is either an extraordinary coincidence or a widely shared urban tale or anxious Jungian dream. Everyone agrees, however, that this is indeed the best of the worst reading stories, that it contains all the excruciating elements of fear and embarrassment inherent in this public occasion for participants who are, by nature, shy of public occasions. When it comes to readings, Martone thinks often of water: water in a cup or bottle the only prop available to the platform reader beyond the pages of the manuscript and the occasion to futz with the microphone. Bottled water seems to be replacing the paper cup or glass tumbler. Bottles have eliminated the need for a pitcher too, which only revealed the degree of nervousness in the tremor of pouring. A glass of water seems more refined than the now more prevalent plastic bottle. The construction of that vessel creates a dramatic gesture. The reader must tip the bottle up completely, one's lips affixed to the narrow opening, manipulating the glugging management of air and liquid, a pantomime of fellation. Martone, unscrewing the cap of the proffered bottle of water at his own readings, can't help but think of that as he tips his head back, the image feeding back to amplify his already active self-consciousness and embarrassment. Water, Martone thinks. As an organizer or host of various series of readings throughout his career, Martone has worried about water—the providing of it and its delivery devices. The task is made most difficult when there is more than one reader. Will the first reader drink out of both glasses thereby "contaminating" the other reader's prepared and waiting glass? Martone has watched (admittedly with some horror) a reader hesitate when deciding which glass to take up, having forgotten where that reader had set down the drink after first imbibing. Martone has watched the looks of consternation cross the faces of readers in that position, gamely attempting to maintain the informative patter between swallows. This confusion does not depend on an evening with two or more readers. Proprietary glasses can be confused simply between the reader and the person introducing the reader who might have his or her own supply of water that is or isn't touched (introductions being relatively short in comparison to the readings themselves). Martone, when it is his role to introduce, usually remembers to take back to his seat his glass or bottle of water after the introduction thereby leaving a clear, unambiguous field of play water-wise, as it were, for the introduced reader. Though this practice, the retrieval of the introducer's water by the introducer once the introduction has been made, creates an additional moment of awkwardness when the introducer and the introducee pass on the stage (one heading back to the seats and the other to the podium) during the obligatory polite applause-covered exchange between the introducer and the reader. The moment is already fraught. A handshake?

A hug? A hug and kiss on the cheek? A high-five? It is the dramatized moment of appreciation for the introduction, a physical launch after the verbal one that has just ended. Martone, in the introductory role, complicates matters when his hands are full at that moment of contact with the notes of his introduction and now the water and its apparatus retrieved to avoid the future confusion of the speaker. Few readers ever finish all their water during their reading. They are good at rationing it out over the course of the evening's performance, not wanting to be caught short during the crucial crescendo moments of the delivery. There is nothing worse than the dry mouth (both the syndrome and the symptom), Martone knows. Martone, in his role as host of a reading, is often faced with what to do with the leftover water of his guests who are (after greeting his or her enthusiastic listeners before the stage, signing some books, and shaking hands) taking off to the evening's reception. Martone is left behind to secure the room, coil the microphone cables, clean up, kill the lights. Part of the cleaning-up part has always included the disposing of the evening's water. Often the lecture halls and auditoriums are not outfitted with a sink. Indeed, the whole point of the headache of providing water in the first place has been the fact that the hall is not in close proximity to sources of water. So Martone has found that he has fallen into the habit of finishing the water himself, drinking the dregs from the glasses or bottles left by the readers like a priest ingesting the leftover Eucharist at the end of Mass. Martone does this more out of a sense of neatness and order but, he supposes, there is some of the spirit involved as well. He has witnessed some really amazing performances, listened to the work of famous and remarkably gifted writers. And he has drunk their leftover water. Perhaps a part of him believes some of that talent and skill will find its way into his own metabolism through this communion with greatness. It is a kind of inoculation, by means of this tainted fluid, with the cooties of the greatest. Martone hopes, as he drinks, that its inspirational properties if not the medicinal ones have "taken."